INTERWEAVE. favorites

SIMPLY MODERN LACE

20 knit projects

editors: **Allison Korleski** *with* **Erica Smith**

associate art director: **Charlene Tiedemann**

cover and interior design: **Katherine Jackson**

photographer: **Joe Hancock** *except where noted*

 Interweave
A division of F+W Media, Inc.
4868 Innovation Drive
Fort Collins, CO 80525
interweave.com

Manufactured in China by RR Donnelley Shenzhen

Library of Congress Cataloging-In-Publication
Data not available at time of printing.
ISBN 978-1-63250-104-2 (pbk)
ISBN 978-1-63250-105-9 (PDF)

10 9 8 7 6 5 4 3 2 1

contents

Introduction

Lace is both fascinating and intimidating to so many knitters. Lace knitting creates some of the loveliest patterns imaginable, but all too often is perceived as difficult—or worse, as dowdy and old-fashioned. Some of the most beautiful lace is actually quite simple; after all, lace is nothing more than strategically placed holes in your knitting, with a corresponding decrease for every yarnover increase. Lace can take center stage in sumptuous shawls and gorgeous sweaters or can serve as an accent, an edging, or an unexpected motif in a sea of stockinette. The craze for small knitted shawls in recent years has led to a new interest in lace knitting, with knitters eager to use it in more modern ways, often paired with stockinette or simple garter stitch.

The projects we've collected here represent the widest variety of lace knitting we could find—from the breathtaking traditional-style shawls many people associate with knitted lace to their more modern, smaller, and simpler counterparts. There are accessories such as hats, socks, and scarves that offer small but satisfying doses of lace knitting, while tops and cardigans give you a choice of challenging (but oh-so-worth-it) allover patterns, or lace used in simple but striking ways—panels, edgings, and simple motifs. Along the way, you'll find useful essays on lace knitting, including a general overview of the technique, an introduction to cast-ons and bind-offs best suited for lace, and how to shape lace patterns.

Whatever your project preference, time allotment, or skill level, you will find projects that will draw you in and get those needles working!

A Primer on Knitted Lace

by Jackie Erickson-Schweitzer

Photos by Jackie Erickson-Schweitzer, *Interweave Knits*, Summer 2006

Airy, light, and a bit mysterious—the delicate tracery of knitted lace is hard to resist. Even the simplest of lace patterns looks impressive and inspires admiration. But intricate as it may appear, knitted lace is simply a fabric punctuated with deliberate openings that can be arranged in a myriad of ways to create patterns that range from basic to complex. The wonderful thing about knitted lace is that in spite of its apparent intricacy, it follows a simple logic. The openings are created by special increases called yarnovers, and each yarnover is accompanied by a compensating decrease. Once you understand how yarnovers and decreases work together, you'll be on your way to mastering the vast array of lace patterns.

Traditional laceweight yarn yields beautiful lace patterns, but sport, worsted, and bulky yarns can be equally effective. A smooth, light-colored fingering or sport-weight yarn worked on a needle three to four sizes larger than you'd normally use creates a fluid fabric in which the lace pattern is clearly visible. But fuzzy yarns and dark and variegated colors yield impressive results, too. Experiment with different yarns and needle sizes when you're swatching lace patterns to see the variety of effects you can create with a single pattern; you'll quickly find out what appeals to you.

GETTING STARTED
YARNOVERS AND DECREASES IN A SIMPLE LACE PATTERN

A yarnover is a stitch made by a loop or strand of yarn placed on the right-hand needle as you work. On the return row, this loop is worked as you would any other stitch; once knitted, it leaves a small opening in the knitting. Each yarnover is counted as an increase of one stitch. To maintain a consistent stitch count, every yarnover is paired with a decrease that may immediately precede or follow the yarnover, appear several stitches away from the yarnover in the same row, or even be worked on a later row. The decreases used in lace knitting are standard: k2tog, ssk, and any of the several kinds of double decreases. The specific kind of decrease to use in any lace pattern is spelled out in its instructions. A good way to see how yarnovers and decreases work together is to knit a sample pattern.

Yarnovers Between Knit Stitches

In the Simple Lace pattern at right, the yarnover is made between two knit stitches and is worked as follows: after knitting the stitch before the yarnover, bring the yarn forward between the needle tips. When you knit the next stitch, bring the yarn up and over the right-hand needle to the back of the work again, ready to knit the next stitch (**Figure 1**). The strand that travels over the top of the needle is the yarnover, and it counts as one stitch.

Figure 1. Yarnover worked between two knit stitches.

Note that in this pattern, you are working the yarnovers and decreases for lace patterning on the right-side rows. The wrong-side return rows are considered "rest rows" because they are worked without any yarnovers or decreases. Although some lace patterns have patterning on every row, it is quite common for lace patterns to have rest rows that alternate with pattern rows.

Check your work often. If you do discover a mistake, correct it right away. (See page 10 for how to fix mistakes.) After you have knitted a few repeats of the pattern, finish with Row 6 of the repeat and bind off loosely. Pin out the swatch, stretching it so that the pattern formed by the holes is clearly visible. Then steam the swatch.

READING A CHART FOR A SIMPLE LACE PATTERN

Instructions for knitted lace are often presented in chart form. Charts offer a graphic representation of the front or right side of the pattern. The chart at right shows a visual picture of the lace-pattern repeat given in the written instructions above.

Simple Lace Pattern

With size 8 needles and fingering yarn (or any yarn and a pair of larger-than-usual needles), loosely cast on 27 sts (or any multiple of 9 stitches, the stitch repeat). You may find it helpful to place markers between each 9-stitch repeat.

Row 1: (RS) *K2, k2tog, yo, k1, yo, ssk, k2; rep from * to end of row.

Rows 2, 4, 6: (WS) Purl.

Row 3: *K1, k2tog, yo, k3, yo, ssk, k1; rep from * to end of row.

Row 5: *K2tog, yo, k1, yo, sl 2 as if to k2tog, k1, pass sl sts over, yo, k1, yo, ssk; rep from * to end of row.

Repeat Rows 1–6 for pattern.

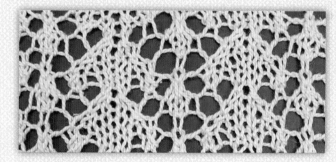

Simple Lace Pattern

Simple Lace Pattern

	k on RS; p on WS
O	yo
/	k2tog
\	ssk
⋀	sl 2 as if to k2tog, k1, p2sso

Each line of the chart represents a row of the stitch pattern. Each square represents a stitch. The chart is read from bottom to top, and RS rows are read from right to left, in the same direction as one normally knits. The first stitch on the left-hand needle as you're ready to begin a row corresponds to the first square in the bottom right-hand corner of the chart. Notice how wrong-side rows have no patterning; they are rest rows. The symbol key tells what to do for each stitch; for example, a plain square represents a knitted stitch and a circle represents a yarnover. A right-slanting line represents k2tog and means that you knit the stitch that corresponds to the k2tog square with the stitch to the left of it.

Note that in this lace pattern, the chart shows that the number of stitches stays the same in each row—for every yarnover, there is a corresponding decrease, and vice versa. On Row 1, the right-slanting k2tog decrease is paired with the yarnover that follows it, and the left-slanting ssk decrease is paired with the yarnover that precedes it. On Row 5, the center double decrease (sl 2 as if to k2tog, k1, pass sl sts over) decreases two stitches, and the yarnovers made on each side of the decrease add two stitches to compensate.

YARNOVERS AND DECREASES IN A BIAS LACE PATTERN

In the Simple Lace pattern, the yarnovers and decreases are balanced. In each repeat, one yarnover falls to the right of its decrease and the other falls to the left of its decrease. Other lace patterns, like the Bias Lace

Bias Lace Pattern

Loosely cast on 28 sts (or any multiple of 7 stitches).

Rows 1, 3, 5, and 7: (RS) *P1, ssk, k2, yo, k1, p1; rep from * to end.

All even-numbered rows (2–16): (WS) *K1, p5, k1; rep from * to end.

Rows 9, 11, 13, and 15: *P1, k1, yo, k2, k2tog, p1; rep from * to end.

Repeat Rows 1–16 for pattern.

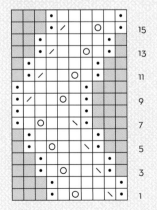

Bias Lace Pattern

Bias Lace Pattern

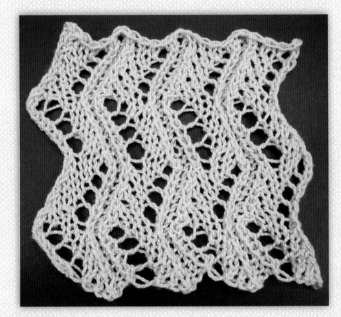

	k on RS; p on WS
•	p on RS; k on WS
O	yo
/	k2tog
\	ssk
	no stitch

Pattern at right, create zigzag patterns by arranging the yarnovers to fall consistently on one side of their corresponding decreases for several rows before reversing the order.

After you have worked several repeats of the pattern, you'll notice that the edges of the sample are wavy, and the stitches tilt away from the vertical to create a bias-lace fabric. The stitches tilt to the right for the first eight rows because the yarnovers' position to the left of their decreases forces the grain of the fabric to lean to the right. At the same time the fabric angles to the left. On the following eight rows, the stitches slant to the left because the yarnovers line up to the right of their decreases, and the edges lean to the right. The cast-on edge is slightly scalloped because the yarnover increases and their compensating decreases are separated by other plain stitches.

For your sample, repeat Rows 1–16 twice, then bind off loosely. Notice that the bound-off edge is also slightly wavy due to this separation of yarnovers and compensating decreases, but the scallop is less pronounced than on the cast-on edge. You can increase the scalloped effect of the bind-off row by binding off in pattern and working the decreases extra tight and the yarnovers and stitches on either side of them extra loose.

READING A CHART FOR A BIAS PATTERN AND "NO-STITCH" SYMBOLS

As mentioned above, one advantage of a lace chart is that it shows a rough picture of the actual knitted fabric. Charts for bias patterns with wavy edges employ a "no-stitch" symbol, which is simply a placeholder that's usually represented by a gray square. You don't do anything when you see a gray no-stitch symbol. You only knit according to the symbols represented by the white squares.

Compare the chart at left to the written instructions for the bias lace pattern. The instructions and the chart tell you how to knit the same lace pattern, but the chart gives a visual picture of how the lace will look.

Besides bias patterns, there are other types of lace that may use the no-stitch symbol in charts. Examples include patterns with stitch counts that vary from row to row (a yarnover's compensating decrease is deferred until a later row in the pattern), some lace edgings, and certain garment shapes.

YARNOVERS WORKED BETWEEN DIFFERENT TYPES OF STITCHES

Whether knits or purls precede or follow a yarnover determine the way it's made. In the Simple Lace pattern, the yarnovers always fall between two knit stitches. The three other yarnovers are made as follows:

Yarnover Between a Knit and a Purl

(Working yarn begins in back.) Bring the yarn to the front of work between needles. Then bring the strand of yarn over the needle and through the needles again to the front—wrapping the needle—and ready to purl the next stitch (**Figure 2**).

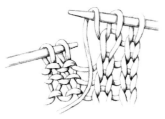

Figure 2. Yarnover worked after a knit and before a purl stitch.

Yarnover Between a Purl and a Knit

(Working yarn begins in front.) Bring the strand of yarn over the right-hand needle to the back and knit the next stitch (**Figure 3**).

Figure 3. Yarnover worked after a purl and before a knit stitch.

Yarnover Between a Purl and a Purl

(Working yarn begins in front.) Bring the strand of yarn over the right-hand needle to the back and to the front again between the tips of the needles—wrapping the needle—ready to purl the next stitch (**Figure 4**).

Figure 4. Yarnover worked between two purl stitches.

Mixed Knit-Purl Lace

To practice the different yarnovers, work this variation of the Simple Lace pattern. Cast on 27 sts (or any multiple of 9 stitches).

Row 1: (RS) *P2, k2tog, yo, p1, yo, ssk, p2; rep from * to end.

Row 2: *K2, p2, k1, p2, k2; rep from * to end.

Row 3: *P1, k2tog, yo, p3, yo, ssk, p1; rep from * to end.

Row 4: *K1, p2, k3, p2, k1; rep from * to end.

Row 5: *K2tog, yo, p1, yo, p3tog, yo, p1, yo, ssk; rep from * to end.

Row 6: *P2, k5, p2; rep from * to end.

Repeat Rows 1–6 for pattern.

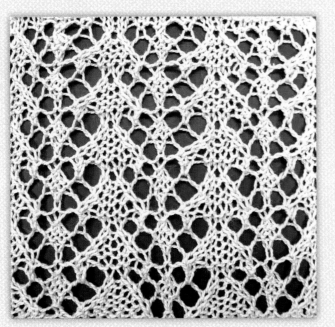

Mixed Knit-Purl Lace

Work the Mixed Knit-Purl Lace pattern to see the variety of yarn-over possibilities. Complete Row 6 of the last pattern repeat and bind off loosely. Block the sample. Compare this variation to the Simple Lace Pattern to see how changing knit stitches to purls varies the pattern.

COMMON MISTAKES AND GETTING BACK ON TRACK

If you discover a mistake, take a breath and stay calm. Even expert knitters make mistakes. The most common mistakes in lace knitting are fairly easy to fix.

* If you forgot to make a yarnover, identify where you omitted the yarnover and temporarily mark that spot with a removable marker or safety pin. On the return row, insert the right-hand needle from back to front under the running thread (the strand directly between and below the two needles), pick it up and place it on the left-hand needle ready to take the place of the missing yarnover.

* If you make an extra yarnover, on the return row drop the extra loop and continue on. At first that area will look a bit looser, but blocking will even out any irregularities.

* If the pattern design doesn't look right or the stitch count is off, and you can't identify the problem, unwork stitches one by one across the row. Recheck your stitch count until you get to a place where the pattern works properly again, then proceed.

Using a Lifeline

A lifeline is a temporary thread inserted through a row of stitches that serves as a checkpoint if you need to rip out and redo several rows. Here's how to make a lifeline:

1. Decide on a lifeline row. A good choice is an unpatterned rest row at the beginning or end of a pattern repeat, for example Row 6 in our first lace-pattern example.

2. After completing the designated row, thread a fine, smooth thread (crochet thread works well) in a contrasting color onto a tapestry needle and run it through the bottom of each stitch on the needle, but not through any markers. Pull the lifeline thread out on each side of the row, leaving tails at least 6" (15 cm) hanging down on each side. When you resume knitting, be careful not to knit the lifeline into the new stitches you make.

With luck, you'll never need to use the lifeline. But if you discover a mistake, remove the knitting needle and ravel down to the lifeline thread. With a smaller size knitting needle, pick up stitches along the lifeline thread by inserting the needle tip through each stitch held by the lifeline; follow the lifeline thread to pick up all the stitches in the original marked row so that they are mounted on the needle properly. Do not remove the lifeline. Count the stitches to be sure that you have the number you should have on the designated lifeline row. Then resume knitting with the original size needles.

Preventing Mistakes

Practicing a few good habits will make it easy to work even the trickiest lace pattern.

- Be sure that you can easily read and keep your place in the instructions. Enlarge charts and, if necessary, transcribe texts or charts into terminology or symbols that work for you.

- Use a magnetic strip, ruler, or Post-it just above the row you are working. Doing so helps your eyes focus on that row while it allows you to check previously knitted rows as a reference point.

- Create good working conditions: increase lighting, minimize distractions, and avoid knitting when you are tired.

- Check your work often: count stitches, use markers liberally, and visually compare your knitting against any available charts and sample photographs.

- Read the pattern out loud as you work through the pattern the first few times. Simultaneous seeing, hearing, and doing can be helpful.

Greenfield
cardigan

---

by **Melissa LaBarre**

This is perhaps the most intriguing project here, as many people who saw it first asked "where is the lace?" Yet while this garter-stitch cardigan is simple to knit, the thoughtful details create an elegant sweater, particularly the lace leaf detail on each front. Top-down raglan construction uses eyelet increases to accent the shaping and echo the lace detail, and the three-quarter length sleeves make it perfect for transitional weather.

Finished Size

36 (40, 44, 48, 52)" (91.5 [101.5, 112, 122, 132] cm) bust circumference, buttoned; cardigan shown measures 36" (91.5 cm).

Yarn

DK (#3 Light).

SHOWN HERE: Shibui Merino Kid (55% kid mohair, 45% merino; 218 yd [199 m]/100 g): #MK7495 wasabi (yellow-green), 4 (5, 6, 7, 8) skeins.

Needles

U.S. size 6 (4 mm): 32" (80 cm) circular (cir) and set of 4 or 5 double-pointed (dpn).

Adjust needle size if necessary to obtain the correct gauge.

Notions

6 markers (m); stitch holders or waste yarn; three ⅞" (2.2 cm) buttons; tapestry needle.

Gauge

20 sts and 32 rows = 4" (10 cm) in garter st.

Cardigan

Neck

With cir needle and using the long-tail method (see Glossary), CO 118 sts. Do not join.

Knit 2 rows.

Shape Back Neck

note: *Do not pick up wraps from short-rows.*

SHORT-ROW 1: (RS) K95, wrap next st, turn (see Glossary).

SHORT-ROW 2: (WS) K72, wrap next st, turn.

NEXT ROW: Knit to end.

NEXT ROW: Knit.

NEXT ROW: (RS; beg buttonhole row) K23, place marker (pm), k14, pm, k44, pm, k14, pm, k18, BO 2 sts, knit to end.

NEXT ROW: (WS; end buttonhole row) K3, use the backward-loop method (see Glossary) to CO 2 sts, knit to end of row.

Shape Raglan

ROW 1: (RS) [Knit to 1 st before m, yo, k1, sl m, k1, yo] 4 times, knit to end of row—8 sts inc'd.

ROW 2: [Knit to 1 st before m, p1, sl m, p1] 4 times, knit to end.

Rep last 2 rows 20 (25, 30, 35, 40) more times, and *at the same time* work buttonhole as before every 20th row 2 more times—286 (326, 366, 406, 446) sts.

Divide for Body and Sleeves

NEXT ROW: (RS) Knit to first m, remove m, place 56 (66, 76, 86, 96) sleeve sts onto holder, remove m, use the backward-loop method to CO 2 (2, 2, 4, 4) sts for underarm, pm, CO 2 (2, 2, 4, 4) sts for underarm, knit to next m, remove m, place 56 (66, 76, 86, 96) sleeve sts onto holder, remove m, use the backward-loop method to CO 2 (2, 2, 4, 4) sts for underarm, pm, CO 2 (2, 2, 4, 4) sts for underarm, knit to end—182 (202, 222, 250, 270) sts rem for body.

Knit 9 rows.

Shape Waist

NEXT ROW: (RS; dec row) *Knit to 6 sts before m, ssk, k4, sl m, k4, k2tog; rep from * once more, knit to end—4 sts dec'd.

Rep dec row every 8th row 3 more times—166 (186, 206, 234, 254) sts rem.

Work 7 rows even.

NEXT ROW: (RS; inc row) *Knit to 5 sts before m, k1f&b (see Glossary), k4, sl m, k4, k1f&b; rep from * once more, knit to end—4 sts inc'd.

Leaf

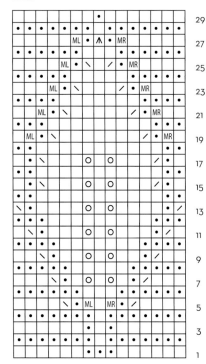

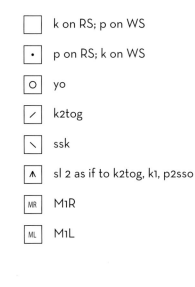

	k on RS; p on WS
•	p on RS; k on WS
O	yo
/	k2tog
\	ssk
⋀	sl 2 as if to k2tog, k1, p2sso
MR	M1R
ML	M1L

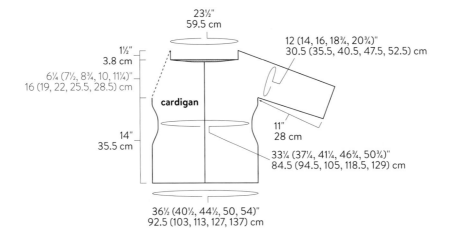

23½"
59.5 cm

1½"
3.8 cm

6¼ (7½, 8¾, 10, 11¼)"
16 (19, 22, 25.5, 28.5) cm

cardigan

14"
35.5 cm

12 (14, 16, 18¾, 20¾)"
30.5 (35.5, 40.5, 47.5, 52.5) cm

11"
28 cm

33¼ (37¼, 41¼, 46¾, 50¾)"
84.5 (94.5, 105, 118.5, 129) cm

36½ (40½, 44½, 50, 54)"
92.5 (103, 113, 127, 137) cm

Rep inc row every 8th row 3 more times—182 (202, 222, 250, 270) sts.

Leaf Motif

Work even until piece measures 10" (25.5 cm) from underarm, ending with a WS row.

NEXT ROW: (RS) K10, pm, work Row 1 of Leaf chart, pm, knit to last 25 sts, pm, work Row 1 of Leaf chart, pm, k10.

Cont in patt through Row 29 of chart.

Cont in garter st until piece measures 14" (35.5 cm) from underarm, ending with a RS row. With WS facing, BO all sts kwise.

Sleeves

Place 56 (66, 76, 86, 96) held sleeve sts onto dpn. Beg at center of underarm, pick up and knit (see Glossary) 2 (2, 2, 4, 4) sts in CO sts, k56 (66, 76, 86, 96), pick up and knit 2 (2, 2, 4, 4) sts in CO sts, pm and join for working in the rnd—60 (70, 80, 94, 104) sts. Work in garter st (knit 1 rnd, purl 1 rnd) until piece measures 11" (28 cm) from underarm, ending with a purl rnd.

BO all sts kwise.

Finishing

With RS facing, pick up and knit 79 (83, 88, 93, 98) sts along center front edge of right front. Knit 2 rows. With WS facing, BO all sts kwise. Rep for left front. Sew buttons to left front opposite buttonholes.

Weave in loose ends. Block to measurements.

Salter Path
shawl

by **Melissa J. Goodale**

*This shawl uses the formulas for a full-*circle shawl and adapts them to create a more modern, wearable semicircle. Inspired by waves washing over the rocks of a tide pool, the color changes in the finished shawl are visually striking, as is the transition from garter stitch to lace.

Finished Size
About 52" (132 cm) wide at top edge and 26" (66 cm) deep.

Yarn
Fingering weight
(#1 Super Fine).

SHOWN HERE: Hazel Knits Artisan Sock (90% wool, 10% nylon; 400 yd [366 m]/120 g): Low Tide (MC), Fudge (CC1), and Beach Glass (CC2), 1 skein each.

Needles
Size U.S. 6 (4 mm): 24" (60 cm) circular (cir).

Adjust needle size if necessary to obtain the correct gauge.

Notions
Tapestry needle.

Gauge
24 stitches and 32 rows = 4" (10 cm) in stockinette stitch; 22 stitches and 27 rows = 4" (10 cm) in garter stitch.

Note
• *This shawl begins with a circular cast-on but is worked back and forth in rows. After casting on, do not draw the loop closed at first. Work back and forth for a few rows before cinching the loop closed.*

Shawl

With CC1, using the Emily Ocker circular beginning (see Glossary and Note), CO 10 sts. Cont with CC1.

NEXT ROW: Sl 1 with yarn in front (wyf), k7, sl 1 wyf, k1, turn.

NEXT ROW: Sl 1 wyf, k1, [k1f&b] 5 times, k1, sl 1 wyf, k1, turn—15 sts.

Arc 1

ROWS 1-3: Sl 1 wyf, k12, sl 1 wyf, k1.

ROW 4: Sl 1 wyf, k1, [k1f&b] 10 times, k1, sl 1 wyf, k1—25 sts.

Arc 2

ROWS 1-5: Sl 1 wyf, k22, sl 1 wyf, k1.

ROW 6: Sl 1 wyf, k1, [k1f&b] 20 times, k1, sl 1 wyf, k1—45 sts.

Arc 3

ROWS 1-11: Sl 1 wyf, k42, sl 1 wyf, k1.

ROW 12: Sl 1 wyf, k1, [k1f&b] 40 times, k1, sl 1 wyf, k1—85 sts.

Arc 4

Change to MC.

ODD ROWS 1-23: Sl 1 wyf, k1, [sl 1 wyf, k4] 16 times, [sl 1 wyf] 2 times, k1.

EVEN ROWS 2-22: Sl 1 wyf, k1, [k1tbl, k4] 16 times, k1tbl, sl 1 wyf, k1.

ROW 24: Sl 1 wyf, k1, [k1tbl, M1, (k1f&b) 4 times] 16 times, k1tbl, sl 1 wyf, k1—165 sts.

Arc 5

ODD ROWS 1-47: Sl 1 wyf, k1, [sl 1 wyf, k9] 16 times, [sl 1 wyf] 2 times, k1.

EVEN ROWS 2-46: Sl 1 wyf, k1, [k1tbl, k9] 16 times, k1tbl, sl 1 wyf, k1.

ROW 48: Sl 1 wyf, k1, [k1tbl, M1, (k1f&b) 9 times] 16 times, k1tbl, sl 1 wyf, k1—325 sts.

Arc 6

ODD ROWS 1-23: Sl 1 wyf, k1, [sl 1 wyf, k19] 16 times, [sl 1 wyf] 2 times, k1.

EVEN ROWS 2-24: Sl 1 wyf, k1, [k1tbl, k19] 16 times, k1tbl, sl 1 wyf, k1.

Lace Section

With CC2, work Rows 1-8 of Lace chart 6 times.

NEXT ROW: With MC, sl 1 wyf, k1, purl to last 2 sts, sl 1 wyf, k1.

NEXT ROW: Sl 1 wyf, knit to last 2 sts, sl 1 wyf, k1.

Rep last row twice more.

NEXT ROW: With CC1, sl 1 wyf, knit to last 2 sts, sl 1 wyf, k1.

Rep last row twice more.

BO ALL STS AS FOLL: *K2tog, slip rem st back to left needle; rep from * until 1 st rem; fasten off last st.

Finishing

Weave in all ends. Block piece to finished measurements.

Lace

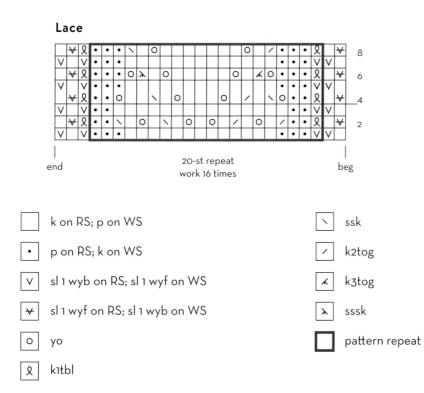

end · 20-st repeat work 16 times · beg

	k on RS; p on WS		\	ssk
·	p on RS; k on WS		/	k2tog
V	sl 1 wyb on RS; sl 1 wyf on WS		⋏	k3tog
Ψ	sl 1 wyf on RS; sl 1 wyb on WS		⋏	sssk
O	yo		▣	pattern repeat
ໃ	k1tbl			

Northampton
neckerchief

by **Cirilia Rose**

This kerchief is a classic square shawl shape but worked on a smaller scale that can be folded into a triangle and tied or pinned for a sweet little accessory or a toasty neck. The lace edging provides a lovely accent, further enhanced by beaded details and a dainty bind-off.

Finished Size
About 30" (76 cm) square, after blocking.

Yarn
Fingering weight
(#1 Super Fine).

SHOWN HERE: Berroco Ultra Alpaca Fine (50% wool, 30% alpaca, 20% nylon; 433 yd [396 m]/100 g): #1293 spiceberry mix (bronze; A), #1284 prune mix (purple; B), and #1282 boysenberry mix (red; C), 1 skein each.

Needles
U.S. size 5 (3.75 mm): set of 5 double-pointed (dpn) and 16" (40 cm) circular (cir).

Adjust needle size if necessary to obtain the correct gauge.

Notions
U.S. size F/5 (3.75 mm) crochet hook; beading needle; 344 size 6° (size E) glass seed beads in gold or amber; 1 locking ring marker (m); 8 markers; digital scale (optional).

Gauge
21 sts and 36 rnds = 4" (10 cm) in St st, after blocking.

Note
• *The yarn requirements will make two kerchiefs. To leave enough yarn for both kerchiefs, use a gram scale to divide each skein into two 50-gram balls.*

Kerchief

A Section

With A and using Emily Ocker's method (see Glossary), CO 12 sts. Divide sts evenly onto 4 dpn. Join for working in the rnd, being careful not to twist sts. Tighten center by tugging on original yarn loop tail.

SET-UP RND: Needle 1: K1, placing locking marker (pm) on this st to mark beg of rnd, pm for patt, yo, k1, yo, pm, k1; Needle 2: K1, pm, yo, k1, yo, pm, k1; Needle 3: K1, pm, yo, k1, yo, pm, k1; Needle 4: K1, pm, yo, k1, yo, pm, k1—20 sts.

Knit 1 rnd.

RND 1: *K1, sl m, yo, knit to m, yo, sl m, k1; rep from * to end—8 sts inc'd.

RND 2: Knit.

Rep Rnds 1 and 2 thirty-three more times, then work Rnd 1 once more—300 sts; 73 sts between markers. **note:** *Change to cir needle when there are too many sts to work comfortably on dpn.*

B Section

Using beading needle, string 140 beads onto B.

NEXT RND: (bead rnd) With B, [k1, sl m, k2, *pb (see Stitch Guide), k1; rep from * to 1 st before m, k1, sl m, k1] 4 times.

With B, work Rnds 1 and 2 (from A section) 15 times, then work Rnd 1 once more—428 sts; 105 sts between markers; B section measures about 3½" (9 cm).

C Section

Using beading needle, string 204 beads onto C. With C, rep bead rnd (from B section). With C, work Rnds 1 and 2 (from A section) 3 times—452 sts; 111 sts between markers. Work lace edging as foll:

RND 1: **K1, sl m, yo, [k1, yo] 2 times, *[ssk] 2 times, sl 2 as if to k2tog, k1, p2sso, [k2tog] 2 times, [yo, k1] 5 times, yo; rep from * to 13 sts before m, [ssk] 2 times, sl 2 as if to k2tog, k1, p2sso, [k2tog] 2 times, [yo, k1] 2 times, yo, sl m, k1; rep from ** to end.

RNDS 2–4: Knit.

Rep last 4 rnds 2 more times.

RND 13: Purl.

RND 14: Knit.

RND 15: Purl.

BO all sts as foll: *Using the cable method (see Glossary), CO 1 st, BO 3 sts, sl st from right needle to left needle; rep from * until all sts have been bound off.

Finishing

Weave in loose ends. Block to measurements.

Knit with a Friend

With the introduction of Ravelry and knitting groups and knitting-based events taking place all over the world, knitting has become a very social activity. This scarf was conceived to be knitted with a friend—the yarn requirements provide enough yardage to make two matching kerchiefs. Use a gram scale to divvy up the yarn prior to knitting to make sure each of you will have enough to complete the project.

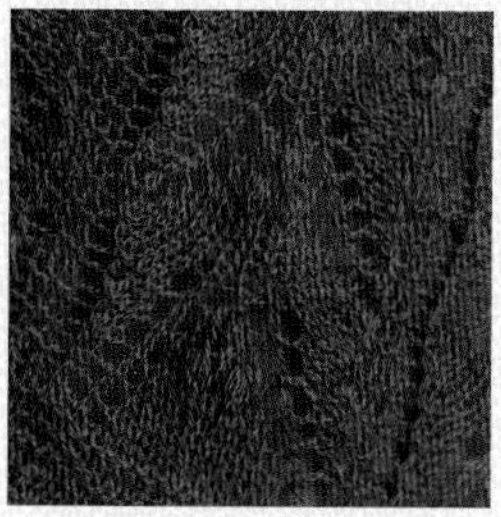

Triinu
scarf

by **Nancy Bush**

Finished Size
About 11" (28 cm) wide and 63" (160 cm) long, after blocking.

Yarn
Fingering weight (#1 Super Fine).

SHOWN HERE: Shelridge Farm Soft Touch Lace, (100% wool; 500 yd [455 m]/50 g): Rust, 1 skein.

Needles
Size U.S. 4 (3.5 mm).

Adjust needle size if necessary to obtain the correct gauge.

Notions
Smooth cotton waste yarn, size G/6 (4.25 mm) crochet hook; markers (m); tapestry needle.

Gauge
11½ stitches and 22 rows = 2" (5 cm) in stockinette stitch, before blocking; 21-stitch pattern repeat of Trinu Center chart measures about 3¼" (8.5 cm) wide, after blocking.

Nancy Bush is arguably the most-recognized master of Estonian knitting techniques. Here she creates a scarf inspired by an article written by Ulle Slamer in an issue of *Triinu* magazine, a publication for Estonians worldwide focusing on traditional customs and culture. The original shawl came as a present from Estonia to a crafts group, but no one had seen the pattern before. Eventually a woman worked it out and wrote a pattern that could be used by other women in the group. The resulting variations demonstrated how traditions survive even as interpretations may change.

7-Stitch Nupp

Working very loosely, work ([k1, yo] 3 times, k1) all in same st—7 nupp sts made from 1 st. On the foll row, purl the 7 nupp sts tog (as shown on chart)—7 nupp sts dec'd back to 1 st.

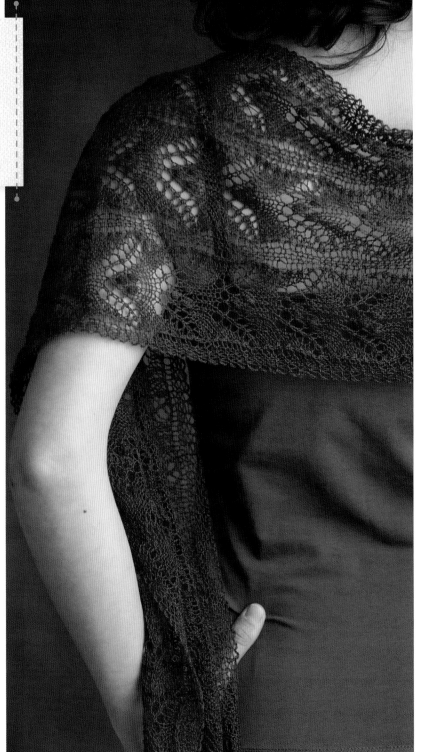

Scarf

With cotton waste yarn and crochet hook, chain about 75 sts (see Glossary). Tie a knot in the end of the cotton after the last chain to identify this end later. With needles and working yarn, pick up and knit 69 sts from the center 69 "bumps" along the back of the crochet chain. Beg and end with a RS row, work 3 rows of garter st, knitting the first st of the first row, but slipping the first st of every row thereafter pwise with yarn in front (wyf).

NEXT ROW: (WS) Sl 1, purl to end.

Change to Triinu Center chart and place markers (pm) after the first 4 sts and before the last 4 sts. Slipping the first st of every row and keeping rem sts outside markers in garter st as shown, rep Rows 1–12 twenty-nine times, or until piece measures about 6½" (16.5 cm) less than desired total length—348 chart rows completed. Slipping the first st of every row, knit 6 rows and *at the same time* inc 22 sts evenly spaced on the last WS row—91 sts. Knit 1 RS row, then purl 1 WS row.

Triinu Center

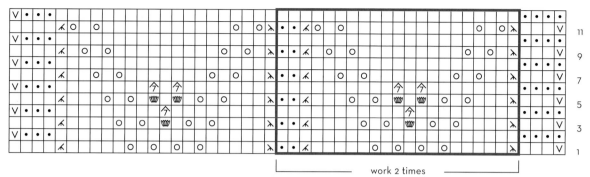

work 2 times

Triinu Lace Edge

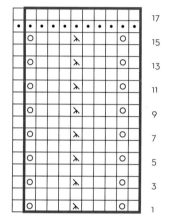

Legend:

- ☐ k on RS; p on WS
- · p on RS; k on WS
- ⊙ yo
- ⟋ k3tog
- ⋋ sl 1, k2tog, psso
- ⏜ 7-st nupp (see Stitch Guide)
- ⤊ p7tog
- v sl 1 (see instructions)
- ☐ pattern repeat

Top Lace Edge

Work Rows 1–17 of Triinu Lace Edge chart.

note: *First st of every row is not slipped for lace edge. With yarn doubled, BO all sts on next WS row.*

Break yarn, leaving a 6" (15 cm) tail.

Bottom Lace Edge

Beg at knotted end, carefully remove the waste-yarn crochet chain, placing each live st on needle as it becomes free—69 sts. If necessary, reorient the sts on the needle so RS of scarf is facing you and join

yarn ready to work a RS row. Knit 2 rows and *at the same time* inc 22 sts evenly spaced on second row—91 sts. Knit 1 RS row, then purl WS 1 row. Work Rows 1–17 of Triinu Lace Edge chart as for top lace edge. With yarn doubled, BO all sts on next WS row. Break yarn, leaving a 6" (15 cm) tail.

Finishing

Handwash gently with mild soap and warm water. Pin scarf out to desired measurements, pinning out each [yo, k1, yo] point in the lace edges. When dry, weave in loose ends.

Beyond the Basics:
Reading Charts

Based on an article by **Ann Budd**

Photos **by Joe Coca**

Many beginning knitters pale at the sight of a charted knitting pattern, temporarily paralyzed by the seemingly complicated abbreviations and symbols (k2tog, ssk, brackets, parentheses, asterisks). But symbol language is actually quite simple; rather than an unbreakable code, it is truly useful shorthand. Curiously, however, many knitters never make the jump to following charted patterns, failing to understand how logical and, yes, easy to follow, they really are.

Charts have several advantages over row-by-row knitting instructions written out in words: They let you see at a glance what's to be done and what the pattern will look like knitted; they help you recognize how the stitches relate to one another; and they take up less space than written instructions. To save space, more and more stitch patterns are charted instead of written out row by row, and that means it is more important than ever to learn how to read them.

THE ANATOMY OF A CHART

Charts are a visual representation of a knitted fabric viewed from the right side. Charts are plotted on graph paper so that one square represents one stitch and one horizontal row represents one row of knitting. The symbols or colors in the squares indicate how to work each stitch. For color-work charts, the colors represent yarn colors. For texture work, the symbols represent stitch manipulations. Some charts include symbols for color as well as stitch manipulations. Unless otherwise specified, charts are read from the bottom to the top; right to left for right-side rows and left to right for wrong-side rows. When knitting in the round (where the right side of the knitting is always facing out), all rows are read from right to left.

The charts in this book are plotted on a square grid. Because knitted stitches tend to be wider than they are tall, motifs worked from these charts will appear somewhat squattier in the actual knitting than they appear on the grid. To avoid this discrepancy when designing your own project, use proportional knitter's graph paper (available at many knitting stores).

Symbols

Though not all publications use exactly the same symbols (for example, some use a horizontal dash to denote a purl stitch, others use a dot), for the most part, the symbols represent what the stitches look like when viewed from the right side of the fabric. Symbols that slant to the left represent left-slanting stitches. Symbols that slant to the right represent right-slanting stitches. Notice how the symbols in the charts on page 31 mimic the

Comparing Charts & Swatches

Notice how the stitches mimic the chart symbols in this simple lace pattern.

The chart symbols for cables indicate the direction of the cable twists.

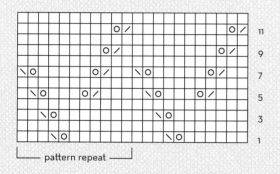

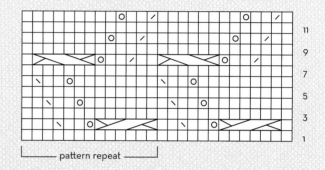

pattern repeat

pattern repeat

Common Chart Symbols & Definitions

	right side: knit, wrong side: purl
·	right side: purl, wrong side: knit
/	right side: k2tog; wrong side: p2tog
⁄	right side: k3tog; wrong side: p3tog
\	right side: ssk; wrong side: ssp
∧	right side: sl 2 sts individually, k1, p2sso wrong side: p2tog and place st onto left needle, pass next st over this st, return st to right needle
M	Make 1
O	yarnover

b	work through back loop of stitch
	no stitch
	Right cross: place specified number of sts onto cable needle and hold in back, knit specified number of sts, knit specified number of sts from cable needle.
	Left cross: place specified number of sts onto cable needle and hold in front, knit specified number of sts, knit specified number of sts from cable needle.

stitches in the knitted fabrics. Think of a knitting chart as a shorthand cartoon representation of the knitted fabric. Each square represents one stitch. The shapes and slants of the symbols imitate the shapes and slants of the knitted stitches.

Because charts are presented as viewed from the right side only, most symbols represent two different maneuvers—one for right-side rows and another for wrong-side rows. For example, for stockinette stitch, you knit the stitches on right-side rows and purl them on wrong-side rows. However, charted stockinette stitch shows only the right, or knit, side. A list of some common symbols and their right- and wrong-side definitions is provided on page 31.

No Stitch

Many stitch patterns, especially lace, involve increases or decreases that cause the stitch count to rise or fall, thereby requiring the number of boxes in a chart to vary from one row to the next. For some patterns, these variations are simply represented by uneven chart edges. For other patterns, adding or subtracting boxes at the edge of a chart may disrupt the vertical stitch alignment in the pattern. In these cases, a special symbol for "no stitch" is used within the borders of the chart so that stitches that are aligned vertically in the knitting are aligned vertically in the chart. The "no stitch" symbol accommodates a "missing" stitch while maintaining the vertical integrity of the pattern. In this book, missing stitches

are represented by gray shaded boxes. When you come to a shaded box, simply skip over it and continue to the end of the row as if it doesn't exist.

Row Numbers

Rows are numbered along the side of most charts, especially long or complicated ones. Row numbers appearing along the right edge denote right-side rows to be read from right to left. Row numbers appearing along the left edge denote wrong-side rows to be read from left to right. For example, if the number 1 is on the right edge of the chart, that and all subsequent odd-numbered rows are right-side rows; all even-numbered rows are worked from the wrong side (from left to right). With few exceptions, charts

Tips for Working with Charts

- If a chart is so small or complicated that it causes your eyes to strain, copy it onto larger graph paper or make a photocopy enlargement. If the chart involves colorwork and you don't have access to a color photocopier, use colored pencils or markers to color in the appropriate boxes.

- Keep your place while working a chart by holding a straightedge or row finder on the chart and using a row counter on your knitting needle. You can place the straightedge either above or below the row you're working on; placing it on the

row above will let you see how the stitches relate to the previous row (the one you just knitted). Once you've worked a couple of repeats from the chart, you may be able to look at your knitting rather than the chart to figure out what comes next.

- If you plan to design a sweater or other piece around a charted design, be sure to center the design over the center stitch of the piece. Otherwise, you will end up with a partial repeat at one edge that isn't mirrored at the other.

in this book designate Row 1 as a right-side row. For some patterns, this necessitates a "set-up row" be worked prior to the first row of the chart to get the stitches in the necessary sequence of knits and purls before the first right-side row of the pattern.

Pattern Repeats

All charts show at least one pattern repeat. If the repeat is complex, more than one repeat is typically charted to help you see how the individual motifs look adjacent to each other.

In row-by-row instructions, pattern repeats are flanked by asterisks or square brackets. On charts, these repeats are outlined in heavy or colored boxes, or they're annotated at the lower or upper edge of the chart.

Some patterns that are worked back and forth in rows require extra stitches to balance a charted pattern. In row-by-row instructions, such patterns are reported as repeating over a multiple of a number of stitches plus extra stitches (i.e., balanced 2x2 ribbing worked back and forth in rows is a multiple of 4 stitches plus 2). On charts, these balancing stitches appear at the right and left margins of the chart, with the repeat clearly marked in between. On right-side rows, work from right to left, working the stitches on the right edge once, then the repeat as many times as necessary, and end by working the stitches on the left edge once. On wrong-side rows, work from left to right, working the stitches on the left edge once, the repeat box as many times as necessary, and end by working the stitches on the right edge once.

Charts for multisize garments will most likely have different numbers of edge stitches for the different sizes. Read the instructions and chart carefully and be sure to begin and end as specified for the size you are making.

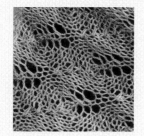

Emily
shawl

by **Mandy Moore**

This sideways-knit shawlette is inlaid with a sweet leaf lace motif. Pointed edges and handpainted silk laceweight yarn make for delicate appeal, while the knitting itself is not so intricate.

Finished Size
About 58" (147.5 cm) wide and 22½" (57 cm) deep at center point, after blocking.

Yarn
Laceweight (#0 Lace).

SHOWN HERE: Blue Moon Fiber Arts Geisha (70% kid mohair, 20% mulberry silk, 10% nylon; 995 yd [910 m]/227 g): jade, 1 skein (this should be enough for three shawls).

Needles
Size U.S. 7 (4.5 mm): 24" (60 cm) or longer circular (cir).

Adjust needle size if necessary to obtain the correct gauge.

Notions
Tapestry needle.

Gauge
20 sts and 20 rows in lace patt = 4¼" (11 cm) wide and 3¼" (8.5 cm) long, after blocking.

Note
• *Blocked gauge will vary throughout piece, as different parts of shawl will be stretched in different ways.*

Shawl

CO 3 sts. Purl 1 row. Work Rows 1–24 of Chart A—15 sts. Work Rows 1–20 of Chart B 3 times—45 sts. Work Rows 1–20 of Chart C 6 times—165 sts. Knit 1 RS row. Using the sewn method (see Glossary), BO all sts.

Finishing

Weave in loose ends. Soak in warm water for 20 min. Squeeze out excess moisture and lay flat on a flat surface to block. Pin corners first, then pin points along shorter straight edges. Points along side edge are formed at the end of each column of yarnovers (end of Row 19 of Charts B and C); points along BO edge are formed at center of each pair of columns of yarnovers. There will be more points along BO edge than side edge. Once all points have been pinned, pin longer curved edge, placing 1 pin every 1–2" (2.5–5 cm). Note that curve may not be symmetrical. Allow to air-dry completely before removing pins.

Chart A

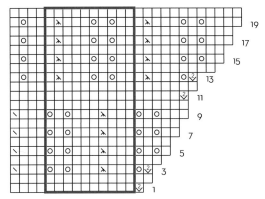

Chart B

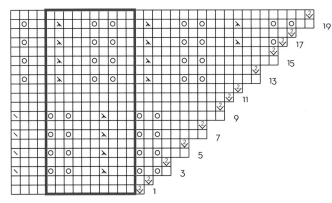

Chart C

☐	k on RS; p on WS
○	yo
\	ssk
⅄	sl 1, k2tog, psso
⤓	k1f&b on RS; p1f&b on WS
☐	pattern repeat

Misty Garden
scarf

by **Jo Sharp**

It's a general rule of thumb that variegated yarns and lace don't get along—the color changes distort or hide the lace patterns and look muddy. Proving the exception to the rule, Jo Sharp's combination of soft modulated colors and a simple feather-and-fan stitch blend harmoniously here, and the finished scarf has a soft painterly feel like an antique watercolor or misty rose garden.

Finished Size
7" (18 cm) wide and 59" (150 cm) long, after blocking.

Yarn
Jo Sharp Rare Comfort Kid Mohair Infusion (80% kid mohair, 15% polyamide, 5% wool; 95 yd [87 m]/25 g): #617 rosehip, 3 balls. Yarn distributed by www.josharp.com.au.

Needles
Size 8 (5 mm).

Adjust needle size if necessary to obtain the correct gauge.

Notions
Tapestry needle.

Gauge
21 sts and 20 rows = 4" (10 cm) in pattern st.

Scarf

CO 38 sts. Work in patt as foll:

ROW 1: (RS) Knit.

ROW 2: Purl.

ROW 3: K1, *[k2tog] 3 times, [yo, k1] 6 times, [k2tog] 3 times; rep from * to last st, k1.

ROW 4: Knit.

Rep Rows 1–4 until piece measures about 59" (150 cm) from beg. BO all sts.

Finishing

Weave in loose ends. Block lightly, if desired.

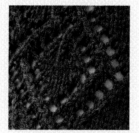

Skyline
tunic

----

by **Melissa Wehrle**; photos by **Heather Weston**

Tunics are one of Melissa Wehrle's favorite wardrobe staples; she calls then "fashionable sweatshirts." The addition of an argyle-like lace panel here makes this tunic a far cry from a sweatshirt, however, and the asymmetric placement takes a classic element and gives it a twist. Like Melissa's native Manhattan skyline, it's stately, artistic, intriguing, and will easily outlast any trend.

Finished Size

34 (36½, 38½, 40½, 44, 48)" (86.5 [92.5, 98, 103, 112, 122] cm) bust circumference. Tunic shown measures 34" (86.5 cm).

Yarn

Worsted weight (#4 Medium).

SHOWN HERE: Valley Yarns Amherst (100% merino wool; 109 yd [100 m]/50 g): charcoal, 10 (11, 11, 12, 13, 14) balls.

Needles

BODY AND SLEEVES: Size U.S. 8 (5 mm): 24" (61 cm) circular (cir) needle.

RIBBING: Size U.S. 7 (4.5 mm): 16" and 24" (40.5 and 61 cm) cir needles.

Adjust needle sizes, if necessary, to obtain the correct gauge.

Notions

Markers (m); stitch holder; tapestry needle.

Gauge

17 sts and 24 rows = 4" (10 cm) in St st on larger needle.

23 sts of Argyle Lace chart measure 5½" (14 cm) wide on larger needle.

Note

- *During shaping, if there are not enough stitches in the chart section to work a decrease with its companion yarnover, work the remaining stitch in stockinette instead.*

STITCH GUIDE

K2, P2 Rib
(multiple of 4 sts + 2)

ROW 1: (RS) K2, *p2, k2; rep from *.

ROW 2: (WS) P2, *k2, p2; rep from *.

Rep Rows 1 and 2 for patt.

Sloped Shoulder Bind-Off
The shoulder stitches are bound off using the sloped shoulder method to eliminate the "stair steps" along the shoulder edge. Work the first BO row as normal, then work 1 row even. On the next BO row, slip the first st knitwise, knit the next st, then pass the slipped st over the knit st to BO 1 st, then work the rest of the BO sts as normal.

Back

With longer cir needle in smaller size, CO 86 (90, 94, 102, 110, 122) sts. Work k2, p2 rib (see Stitch Guide) until piece measures 4" (10 cm), ending with a WS row. Change to larger cir needle, and cont in St st as foll:

NEXT ROW: (RS) K6 (10, 4, 6, 2, 10), [k2tog, k6 (6, 7, 6, 7, 6)] 10 (10, 10, 12, 12, 14) times—76 (80, 84, 90, 98, 108) sts.

Work even in St st until piece measures 7" (18 cm) from CO, ending with a WS row.

Shape Waist

DEC ROW: (RS) K1, ssk (see Glossary), work to last 3 sts, k2tog, k1—2 sts dec'd.

Cont in St st, rep the dec row every 6 (6, 6, 4, 6, 4) rows 6 (6, 5,

2, 4, 1) more time(s), then every 0 (0, 8, 6, 8, 6) rows 0 (0, 1, 5, 2, 6) time(s)—62 (66, 70, 74, 84, 92) sts rem; piece measures about 13¼ (13¼, 13½, 13½, 13¾, 13¾)" (33.5 [33.5, 34.5, 34.5, 35, 35] cm) from CO. Work even for 7 rows, beg and ending with a WS row.

INC ROW: (RS) K1, M1 (see Glossary), work to last st, M1, k1—2 sts inc'd.

Cont in St st, rep the inc row every 8 (6, 6, 6, 8, 8) rows 4 (4, 4, 4, 3, 3)

more times, then every 0 (8, 8, 8, 10, 10) rows 0 (1, 1, 1, 1, 1) time(s)—72 (78, 82, 86, 94, 102) sts. Work even until piece measures 20½ (20½, 21, 21, 21½, 21½)" (52 [52, 53.5, 53.5, 54.5, 54.5] cm) from CO ending with a WS row.

Shape Armholes

BO 4 (5, 6, 6, 7, 9) sts at beg of next 2 rows—64 (68, 70, 74, 80, 84) sts. Dec 1 st at each side every row 4 (4, 4, 5, 6, 6) times—56 (60, 62, 64, 68, 72) sts rem. Work even until armholes measure 7¾ (8, 8¼, 8½, 8¾, 9)" (19.5 [20.5, 21, 21.5, 22, 23] cm), ending with a WS row.

Shape Shoulders and Back Neck

note: *During the following shaping, use the sloped shoulder bind-off method (see Stitch Guide), if desired.*

NEXT ROW: (RS) BO 4 (5, 5, 5, 6, 6) sts, knit until there are 11 (11, 12, 12, 13, 15) sts on right needle after BO, place rem 41 (44, 45, 47, 49, 51) sts on holder—11 (11, 12, 12, 13, 15) right shoulder sts rem on needle.

Right Back Shoulder

NEXT ROW: (WS) P2tog at neck edge, work to end—10 (10, 11, 11, 12, 14) sts.

NEXT ROW: (RS) BO 4 (5, 5, 5, 6, 6) sts, work to last 2 sts, k2tog—5 (4, 5, 5, 5, 7) sts.

NEXT ROW: Work even.

BO rem sts with RS facing.

Left Back Shoulder

Return 41 (44, 45, 47, 49, 51) held sts to needle and rejoin yarn with RS facing.

NEXT ROW: (RS) BO 26 (28, 28, 30, 30, 30) back neck sts, work to end—15 (16, 17, 17, 19, 21) sts.

NEXT ROW: (WS) BO 4 (5, 5, 5, 6, 6) sts, work to last 2 sts, ssp (see Glossary) at neck edge—10 (10, 11, 11, 12, 14) sts.

NEXT ROW: Ssk (see Glossary), work to end—9 (9, 10, 10, 11, 13) sts.

NEXT ROW: BO 4 (5, 5, 5, 6, 6) sts, work to end—5 (4, 5, 5, 5, 7) sts.

NEXT ROW: Work even.

BO rem sts with RS facing.

Front

With longer cir needle in smaller size, CO 86 (90, 94, 102, 110, 122) sts. Work k2, p2 rib until piece measures 4" (10 cm), ending with a WS row. Change to larger cir needle, and cont in St st as foll:

NEXT ROW: (RS) K6 (10, 4, 6, 2, 10), [k2tog, k6 (6, 7, 6, 7, 6)] 10 (10, 10, 12, 12, 14) times—76 (80, 84, 90, 98, 108) sts.

NEXT ROW: (WS) Purl.

NEXT ROW: K11 (12, 13, 14, 17, 20), place marker (pm), work Row 1 of

Argyle Lace

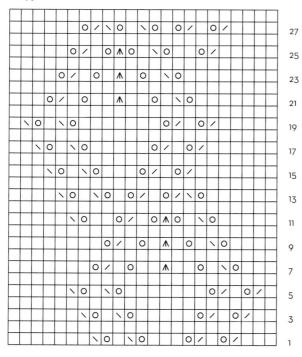

23 sts

knit on RS; purl on WS

/ k2tog

\ ssk

∧ sl 2 as if to k2tog, k1, p2sso

O yo

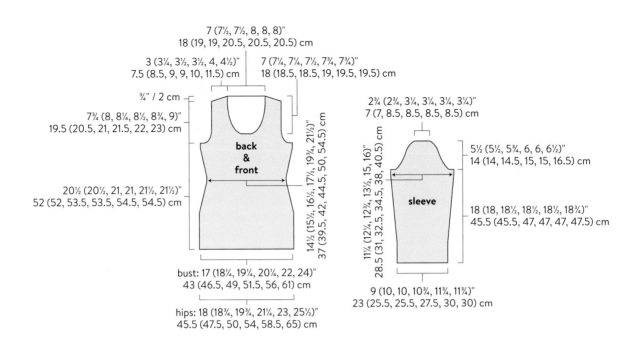

Diagram measurements:

7 (7½, 7½, 8, 8, 8)"
18 (19, 19, 20.5, 20.5, 20.5) cm

3 (3¼, 3½, 3½, 4, 4½)"
7.5 (8.5, 9, 9, 10, 11.5) cm

7 (7¼, 7¼, 7½, 7¾, 7¾)"
18 (18.5, 18.5, 19, 19.5, 19.5) cm

¾" / 2 cm

7¾ (8, 8¼, 8½, 8¾, 9)"
19.5 (20.5, 21, 21.5, 22, 23) cm

back & front

20½ (20½, 21, 21, 21½, 21½)"
52 (52, 53.5, 53.5, 54.5, 54.5) cm

14½ (15½, 16½, 17½, 19¾, 21½)"
37 (39.5, 42, 44.5, 50, 54.5) cm

bust: 17 (18¼, 19¼, 20¼, 22, 24)"
43 (46.5, 49, 51.5, 56, 61) cm

hips: 18 (18¾, 19¾, 21¼, 23, 25½)"
45.5 (47.5, 50, 54, 58.5, 65) cm

2¾ (2¾, 3¼, 3¼, 3¼, 3¼)"
7 (7, 8.5, 8.5, 8.5, 8.5) cm

5½ (5½, 5¾, 6, 6, 6½)"
14 (14, 14.5, 15, 15, 16.5) cm

sleeve

11¼ (12¼, 12¾, 13½, 15, 16)"
28.5 (31, 32.5, 34.5, 38, 40.5) cm

18 (18, 18½, 18½, 18½, 18¾)"
45.5 (45.5, 47, 47, 47, 47.5) cm

9 (10, 10, 10¾, 11¾, 11¾)"
23 (25.5, 25.5, 27.5, 30, 30) cm

Argyle Lace chart over 23 sts, pm, k42 (45, 48, 53, 58, 65).

Working sts outside chart section in St st, cont in patt until piece measures 7" (18 cm) from CO, ending with a WS row.

Shape Waist

Cont in patt, shape waist as for back—72 (78, 82, 86, 94, 102) sts. Work even until piece measures 20½ (20½, 21, 21, 21½, 21½)" (52 [52, 53.5, 53.5, 54.5, 54.5] cm) from CO ending with a WS row.

Shape Armholes

Cont in patt (see Note), work as for back—56 (60, 62, 64, 68, 72) sts rem; armholes measure about 1 (1, 1, 1¼, 1½, 1½)" (2.5 [2.5, 2.5, 3.2, 3.8, 3.8] cm). Work even until armholes measure 1½ (1½, 1¾, 1¾, 1¾, 2)" (3.8 [3.8, 4.5, 4.5, 4.5, 5] cm), ending with a WS row.

Shape Front Neck and Shoulders

NEXT ROW: (RS) Work 24 (26, 27, 28, 30, 32) sts in patt and place sts just worked on holder for left neck, BO 8 center front sts, k24 (26, 27, 28, 30, 32)—24 (26, 27, 28, 30, 32) right neck sts rem on needle.

Right Front Neck and Shoulder

NEXT ROW: (WS) Work to last 2 sts, ssp at neck edge—1 st dec'd.

NEXT ROW: (RS) Ssk, work to end—1 st dec'd.

Dec 1 st at neck edge (beg of RS rows, end of WS rows) in this manner every row 4 more times, then every RS row 2 times, then every 4 rows 3 (4, 4, 5, 5, 5) times—13 (14, 15, 15, 17, 19) sts rem. Work even until armhole measures 7¾ (8, 8¼, 8½, 8¾, 9)" (19.5 [20.5, 21, 21.5, 22, 23] cm), ending with a RS row. BO 4 (5, 5, 5, 6, 6) sts at beg of next 2 WS rows, then BO 5 (4, 5, 5, 5, 7) sts at beg of foll WS row—no sts rem.

Left Front Neck and Shoulder

Return 24 (26, 27, 28, 30, 32) held sts to needle and rejoin yarn with WS facing.

NEXT ROW: (WS) P2tog at neck edge, work to end—1 st dec'd.

NEXT ROW: (RS) Work to last 2 sts, k2tog—1 st dec'd.

Dec 1 st at neck edge (end of RS rows, beg of WS rows) in this manner every row 4 more times, then every RS row 2 times, then every 4 rows 3 (4, 4, 5, 5, 5) times—13 (14, 15, 15, 17, 19) sts rem. Work even until armhole measures 7¾ (8, 8¼, 8½, 8¾, 9)" (19.5 [20.5, 21, 21.5, 22, 23] cm), ending with a WS row. BO 4 (5, 5, 5, 6, 6) sts at beg of next 2 RS rows, then BO 5 (4, 5, 5, 5, 7) sts at beg of foll RS row—no sts rem.

Sleeves

With longer cir needle in smaller size, CO 38 (42, 42, 46, 50, 50) sts. Work k2, p2 until piece measures 4" (10 cm), ending with a WS row. Change to larger cir needle, and cont in St st as foll:

INC ROW: (RS) K1, M1 (see Glossary), work to last st, M1, k1—2 sts inc'd.

Cont in St st, rep the inc row every 14 (18, 16, 16, 12, 10) rows 4 (4, 5, 5, 6, 8) more times, working new sts in St st—48 (52, 54, 58, 64, 68) sts. Work even until piece measures 18 (18, 18½, 18½, 18½, 18¾)" (45.5 [45.5, 47, 47, 47, 47.5] cm) from CO, ending with a WS row.

Shape Sleeve Cap

BO 4 (5, 6, 6, 7, 9) sts at beg of next 2 rows—40 (42, 42, 46, 50, 50) sts. Dec 1 st at each side every RS row 2 (2, 2, 2, 3, 3) times, then every 4 rows 4 (4, 5, 5, 3, 4) times, then every RS row 4 (3, 3, 3, 6, 6) times, then every row 1 (3, 1, 3, 3, 2) time(s)—18 (18, 20, 20, 20, 20) sts rem. BO 3 sts at the beginning of the next 2 rows—12 (12, 14, 14, 14, 14) sts. BO rem sts.

Finishing

Block pieces to measurements. With yarn threaded on a tapestry needle, sew shoulder seams. Sew sleeves into armholes. Sew sleeve and side seams.

Neckband

With shorter cir needle in smaller size and RS facing, pick up and knit 104 (112, 112, 120, 120, 120) sts around neck opening. Pm and join for working in rnds.

NEXT RND: *K2, p2; rep from *.

Rep the last rnd 6 more times. BO all sts in rib patt.

Weave in all loose ends.

Leaves Long
beanie

by **Melissa LaBarre**

Here's a perfect lace knitting project for beginners. Simple little leaves travel across a garter-stitch background and flow neatly into the decreases in this elongated beanie. Wear it slouched back on your head in the fall or pull it down over your ears when the weather grows colder. The garter-stitch background highlights the color variation of this semisolid yarn.

Finished Size
17¼" (44 cm) circumference at brim; to fit 18–22½" (45.5–57 cm) head circumference.

Yarn
Worsted weight (#4 Medium).

SHOWN HERE: Madelinetosh Vintage (100% superwash merino; 200 yd [183 m]/100 g): nectar, 1 skein.

Needles
RIBBING: U.S. size 5 (3.75 mm): 16" (40 cm) circular (cir) needle.

BODY: U.S. size 7 (4.5 mm): 16" (40 cm) cir needle and set of 4 double-pointed (dpn).

Adjust needle sizes if necessary to obtain the correct gauge.

Notions
Stitch marker (m); tapestry needle.

Gauge
20 sts and 36 rnd = 4" (10 cm) in garter st; 21 sts and 32 rnds = 4" (10 cm) in k1, p1 ribbing, unstretched, with smaller needle.

Ribbing

With smaller cir needle, CO 90 sts. Place marker (pm) for beg of rnd and join for working in the rnd, being careful not to twist sts.

RND 1: *K1, p1; rep from * to end. Rep the previous rnd 9 more times.

Body

Switch to larger cir needle. Work Garter Leaf chart 2 times (48 rnds).

Shape Crown

note: *Change to dpns when there are too few sts to work comfortably on cir needle.*

Work 15 rnds of Decrease chart— 10 sts rem.

NEXT RND: (dec rnd) *K2tog; rep from * to end—5 sts rem.

Break yarn, leaving an 8" (20.5 cm) tail. With tail threaded on tapestry needle, draw through rem sts, pull snug to tighten, and fasten off inside.

Finishing

Weave in ends. Block hat using preferred method.

Using Stitch Markers to Keep Track of Pattern Repeats

When a stitch pattern is repeated several times around the circumference of a hat, it can sometimes be difficult to keep track of where you are in the pattern. If you find that you tend to lose your place, try placing contrasting stitch markers after each pattern repeat. This way, you can catch errors within each repeat, rather than reaching the end of a row and finding that you have too many or too few stitches to complete the pattern.

Garter Leaf

Decrease

- ☐ knit
- ⚫ purl
- ╱ k2tog
- ╲ ssk
- ◎ yo
- ⋀ sl 2, k1, p2sso
- ▨ no stitch
- ☐ pattern repeat

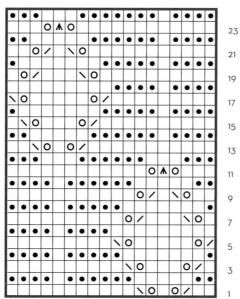

23
21
19
17
15
13
11
9
7
5
3
1

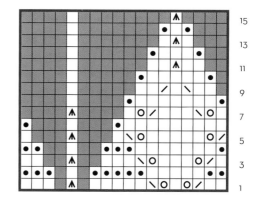

15
13
11
9
7
5
3
1

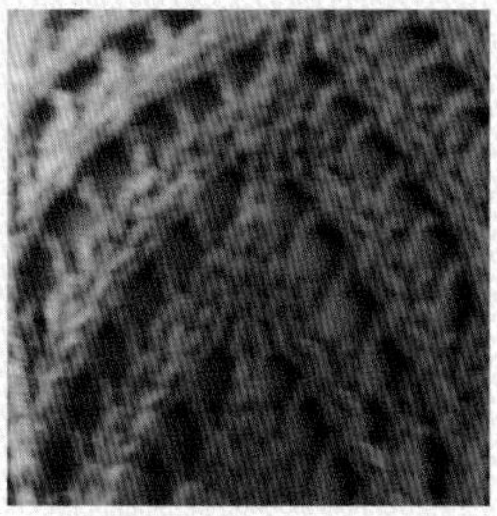

Lace
cardigan

- -

by **Simona Merchant-Dest**

Simona Merchant-Dest's masterpiece is a true challenge, but one well worth the time and effort, and one that will make avid lace knitters swoon with delight. Constructed seamlessly from the top down and shaped along raglan lines, this classic cardigan features a beautiful chandelier lace pattern in the main body, combined with a smaller lace pattern along the center of each sleeve. Stitches are picked up along the center front selvedges, and the bands are worked perpendicular to the body.

Finished Size

About 35 (37, 41, 43, 47, 49, 53)" (89 [94, 104, 109, 119.5, 124.5, 134.5] cm) bust circumference, buttoned, including ½" (1.3 cm) front band. Cardigan shown measures 35" (89 cm).

Yarn

Sportweight (#2 Fine).

SHOWN HERE: Bijou Basin Ranch Lhasa Wilderness (75% yak, 25% bamboo; 180 yd [165 m]/2 oz [56 g]): #05 salmonberry, 5 (6, 6, 7, 7, 7, 8) skeins.

Needles

BODY AND SLEEVES: Size U.S. 3 (3.25 mm): 32" and 16" (80 and 40 cm) circular (cir) and set of 4 or 5 double-pointed (dpn).

WAIST AND SLEEVE HEMS: Size U.S. 2 (2.75 mm): 32" (80 cm) cir and set of 4 or 5 dpn.

Adjust needle sizes if necessary to obtain the correct gauge.

Notions

Markers (m); stitch holders; tapestry needle; nine ⅝" (1.5 cm) buttons.

Gauge

24 sts and 34 rows/rnds = 4" (10 cm) in St st on larger needles.

24 sts and 34 rows = 4" (10 cm) in patt from Chandelier chart on larger needle.

Notes

- The cardigan yoke is worked in one piece from the neck down to the underarms, then the sleeve stitches are placed on holders. The fronts and back are worked back and forth in rows in a single piece to the lower edge. After completing the lower body, the sleeves are worked in rounds to the cuffs.

- In Row 31 of the Chandelier chart (page 56), the beginning or ending point for some sizes does not permit the double decrease to be worked with both its yarnovers. If this occurs at the start of the pattern, work the first 2 pattern stitches as "ssk, yo" instead. If this occurs at the end of the pattern, work the last 2 stitches as "yo, k2tog" instead.

- When joining the fronts and back for the lower body, it is sometimes not possible to add full pattern repeats (for invisible insertion) at the underarms to keep the pattern continuous all the way around the body. In this case, side panels can be inserted in a different pattern to make up the desired circumference.

- You can create a side insert panel that complements the main pattern by isolating one motif or section of the main stitch pattern and using it for the insert. Make a separate chart for the insert pattern that contains the same number of rows or rounds as the main stitch pattern, if possible, to make it easier to keep track of the patterns.

- When calculating the number of lower body stitches, remember to add 1 selvedge stitch at each front edge for a cardigan to make it easier to pick up the front band stitches. In this project, the selvedge stitches are shown on the Right Front and Left Front charts where they are worked in garter stitch (knit every row) at the front edges.

Yoke

With longer cir needle in larger size, CO 101 (101, 101, 101, 119, 119, 119) sts. Do not join.

SET-UP ROW: (WS) P5 for right front, place marker (pm), p25 for right sleeve, pm, p41 (41, 41, 41, 59, 59, 59) for back, pm, p25 for left sleeve, pm, p5 for left front.

note: *For the following instructions, use the Left Front and Right Front charts for your size. See pages 58–61 for charts.*

NEXT ROW: (RS) Inc as shown on charts, work Row 1 of Left Front chart for your size to m, slip marker (sl m), *k1tbl, M1L (see Glossary), k2, pm, work Row 1 of Sleeve chart over 19 sts, pm, k2, M1R (see Glossary), k1tbl, sl m,* work Row 1 of Back chart to m working 18-st patt rep 2 (2, 2, 2, 3, 3, 3) times, sl m; rep from * to * for second sleeve, work Row 1 of Right Front chart for your size to end—111 (111, 111, 111, 129, 129, 129) sts total: 7 sts for each front, 27 sts for each sleeve, 43 (43, 43, 43, 61, 61, 61) sts for back.

NEXT ROW: (WS) Work next row of Right Front chart to m, sl m, *p1tbl, purl to m, sl m, work next row of Sleeve chart over 19 sts, sl m, purl to 1 st before m, p1tbl, sl m,* work next row of Back chart to m, sl m; rep from * to * for second sleeve, work next row of Left Front chart to end.

NECK AND RAGLAN INC ROW: (RS) Work next row of Left Front chart to m, sl m, *k1tbl, M1L, knit to next m, sl m, work next row of Sleeve chart over 19 sts, sl m, knit to 1 st before next m, M1R, k1tbl, sl m,* work next row of Back chart to m, sl m; rep from * to * once more for second sleeve, work next row of Right Front chart to end—10 sts inc'd: 2 sts each for each front, each sleeve, and back.

Cont in patt, rep the shaping of the last 2 rows 6 more times, ending with a RS inc row (Row 15 of fronts and back)—181 (181, 181, 181, 199, 199, 199) sts total: 21 sts each front, 41 sts each sleeve, 57 (57, 57, 57, 75, 75, 75) back sts.

NEXT ROW: (WS; Row 16 of fronts and back) Use the knitted method (see Glossary) to CO 9 (9, 9, 9, 18, 18, 18) sts at right front edge, work across new sts as k1, p8 (8, 8, 8, 17, 17, 17) as shown on Right Front chart, *p1tbl, purl to m, sl m, work next row of Sleeve chart over 19 sts, sl m, purl to 1 st before m, p1tbl, sl m,* work next row of Back chart; rep from * to * for second sleeve, work next row of Left Front chart to end, use the knitted method to CO 9 (9, 9, 9, 18, 18, 18) more sts at left front edge as shown on chart—199 (199, 199, 199, 235, 235, 235) sts total: 30 (30, 30, 30, 39, 39, 39) sts for each front, no change to sleeve and back sts; piece measures 2" (5 cm) from CO.

note: *In this row, the new sts on the Left Front chart are shown using the CO symbol because they have not been worked yet.*

RAGLAN INC ROW: (RS) Work next row of Left Front chart to m, sl m, *k1tbl, M1L, knit to next m, sl m, work next row of Sleeve chart over 19 sts, sl m, knit to 1 st before next m, M1R, k1tbl, sl m,* work next row of Back chart to m, sl m; rep from * to * once more for second sleeve, work next row of Right Front chart to end—8 sts inc'd: 1 st at raglan edge of each front, 2 sts each sleeve, 2 back sts.

NEXT ROW: (WS) Work next row of Right Front chart to m, sl m, *p1tbl, purl to next m, sl m, work next row of Sleeve chart over 19 sts, sl m, purl to 1 st before next m, p1tbl, sl m,* work next row of Back chart to m, sl m; rep from * to * once more for second sleeve, work next row of Left Front chart to end.

Cont in patt, rep the shaping of the last 2 rows 14 (15, 16, 14, 19, 20, 21) more times, then work the raglan

inc row one more time, working new sleeve sts in St st—327 (335, 343, 327, 403, 411, 419) sts total: 46 (47, 48, 46, 60, 61, 62) sts each front, 73 (75, 77, 73, 83, 85, 87) sts each sleeve, 89 (91, 93, 89, 117, 119, 121) back sts. Cont for your size as foll:

Sizes 35 (37, 41, 47)" Only

Yoke shaping is complete, ending with RS Row 47 (49, 51, 57) of front and back charts—piece measures 5½ (5¾, 6, 6¾)" (14 [14.5, 15, 17] cm) from CO, including set-up row.

Sizes (43, 49, 53)" Only

Cont in patt, inc for front and back raglans without working any sleeve incs as foll:

NEXT ROW: (WS) Work 1 WS row even as established.

NEXT ROW: (RS) Work next row of Left Front chart to m, sl m, *k1tbl, knit to next m, sl m, work next row of Sleeve chart over 19 sts, sl m, knit to 1 st before next m, k1tbl, sl m,* work next row of Back chart to m, sl m; rep from * to * once more for second sleeve, work next row of Right Front chart to end— 4 sts inc'd: 1 st each front, 2 back sts, no change to sleeve sts.

Rep the last 2 rows (2, 0, 1) more time(s), ending with RS Row (53, 61, 65) of front and back charts—(339, 415, 427) sts total: (49, 62, 64) sts each front, (73, 85, 87) sts each sleeve, (95, 121, 125) back sts; piece measures (6¼, 7¼, 7¾)" (16 [18.5, 19.5] cm) from CO.

Divide for Body and Sleeves

DIVIDING ROW: (WS; Row 48 [50, 52, 54, 58, 62, 66] of front and back charts) Working next WS chart row as established, work 46 (47, 48, 49, 60, 62, 64) right front sts, put next 73 (75, 77, 73, 83, 85, 87) sleeve sts

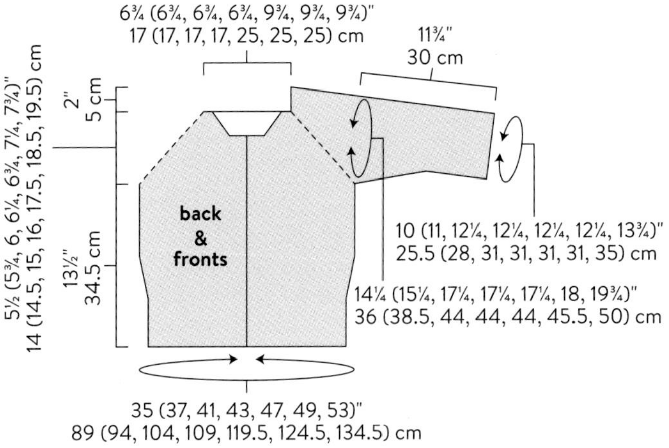
6¾ (6¾, 6¾, 6¾, 9¾, 9¾, 9¾)"
17 (17, 17, 17, 25, 25, 25) cm
11¾"
30 cm
5½ (5¾, 6, 6¼, 6¾, 7¼, 7¾)"
14 (14.5, 15, 16, 17.5, 18.5, 19.5) cm
2"
5 cm
13½"
34.5 cm
back
&
fronts
10 (11, 12¼, 12¼, 12¼, 12¼, 13¾)"
25.5 (28, 31, 31, 31, 31, 35) cm
14¼ (15¼, 17¼, 17¼, 17¼, 18, 19¾)"
36 (38.5, 44, 44, 44, 45.5, 50) cm
35 (37, 41, 43, 47, 49, 53)"
89 (94, 104, 109, 119.5, 124.5, 134.5) cm

Symbol	Meaning
□	knit on RS rows and all rnds; purl on WS rows
•	purl on RS rows and all rnds; knit on WS rows
ℓ	k1tbl on RS rows and all rnds; p1tbl on WS rows
O	yo
/	k2tog
\	ssk
∧	sl 2, k1, p2sso (see Stitch Guide)
R	M1R (see Glossary)
L	M1L (see Glossary)
+	cast-on st
(shaded)	no stitch
(bold box)	pattern repeat

onto waste yarn or holder leaving Sleeve chart m in place, use the knitted method to CO 6 (8, 13, 15, 10, 11, 15) underarm sts, pm for side "seam," CO 7 (9, 14, 16, 11, 12, 16) more underarm sts, work 89 (91, 93, 95, 117, 121, 125) back sts, put next 73 (75, 77, 73, 83, 85, 87) sleeve sts onto waste yarn or holder leaving Sleeve chart m in place, CO 7 (9, 14, 16, 11, 12, 16) underarm sts, pm for side "seam," CO 6 (8, 13, 15, 10, 11, 15) underarm sts, work 46 (47, 48, 49, 60, 62, 64) right front sts—207 (219, 243, 255, 279, 291, 315) sts total: 52 (55, 61, 64, 70, 73, 79) sts each front, 103 (109, 121, 127, 139, 145, 157) back sts.

note: *Record the WS row of the Sleeve chart just completed so you can resume the patt with the correct row later.*

Body

Work for your size as foll:

Sizes 35 (41, 47, 53)" Only

NEXT ROW: (RS) K1 (selvedge st; knit every row as established), beg and ending as indicated for your size, work Row 17 (21, 27, 3) of Chandelier chart over 46 (55, 64, 73) left front sts, *place new m, work Row 1 of Side Insert chart over 11 sts removing side m, then place new m,* work Row 17 (21, 27, 3) of Chandelier chart over 91 (109, 127, 145) back sts beg and ending where indicated for your size; rep from * to * once more for second side panel, work Row 17 (21, 27, 3) of Chandelier chart over 46 (55, 64, 73) right front sts beg and ending where indicated for your size, k1 (selvedge st; knit every row as established).

Work even in established patts until piece measures 6" (15 cm) from dividing row. Change to smaller cir needle. Work even in patts until 79 (75, 85, 77) lower body rows total have been completed, ending with Row 31 (31, 15, 15) of Chandelier chart—piece measures about 9¼ (8¾, 10, 9)" (23.5 [22, 25.5, 23] cm) from dividing row.

Sizes (37, 43, 49)" Only

NEXT ROW: K1 (selvedge st; knit every row as established), beg and ending as indicated for your sizes, work Row (19, 23, 31) of Chandelier chart over center (217, 253, 289) sts, k1 (selvedge st, knit every row as established).

Work even in established patts until piece measures 6" (15 cm) from dividing row. Change to smaller cir needle. Work even in patts until (77, 73, 81) lower body rows total have been completed, ending with Row (31, 31, 15) of Chandelier chart—piece measures about (9, 8½, 9½)" ([23, 21.5, 24] cm) from dividing row.

All Sizes

NEXT ROW: (WS) Purl and *at the same time* dec 3 sts evenly spaced—204 (216, 240, 252, 276, 288, 312) sts rem.

Change to larger cir needle and work in k2, p2 rib (see Stitch Guide) beg with RS Row 2 until piece measures 13½" (34.5 cm) from dividing row for all sizes, ending with a WS row. With RS facing, BO all sts in patt.

Sleeves

note: *The sleeves are worked in rnds, beg with the next odd-numbered chart row after the WS dividing row. When working in rnds, read all even-numbered chart rows as right-side (RS) rnds.*

With shorter cir needle in larger size and RS facing, join yarn to

Back

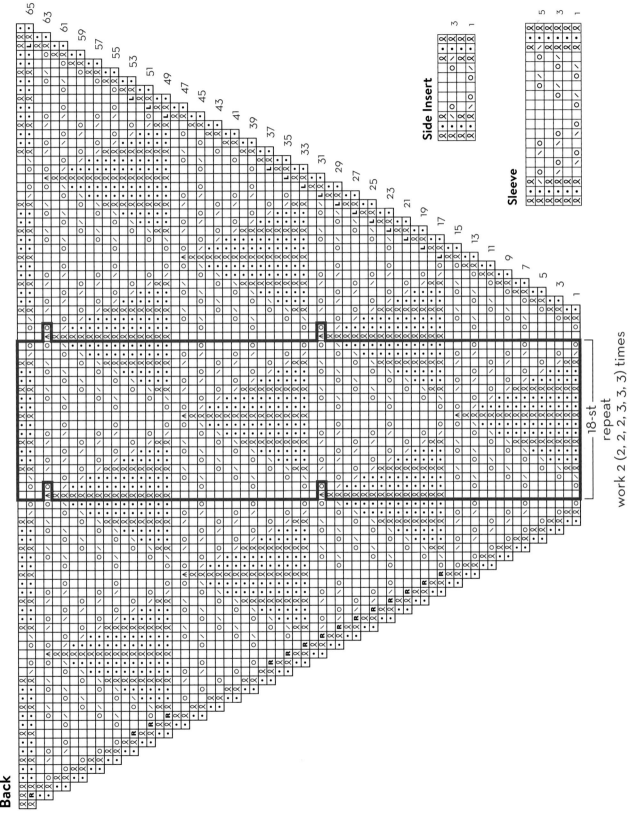

Side Insert

Sleeve

18-st
repeat
work 2 (2, 2, 3, 3, 3) times

Chandelier

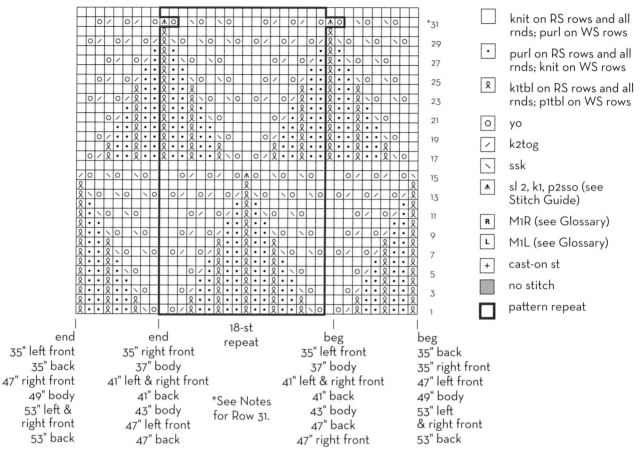

Chart legend:

- ☐ knit on RS rows and all rnds; purl on WS rows
- • purl on RS rows and all rnds; knit on WS rows
- ℚ k1tbl on RS rows and all rnds; p1tbl on WS rows
- o yo
- / k2tog
- \ ssk
- ∧ sl 2, k1, p2sso (see Stitch Guide)
- R M1R (see Glossary)
- L M1L (see Glossary)
- + cast-on st
- ▨ no stitch
- ☐ pattern repeat

Chart row labels (right side): *31, 29, 27, 25, 23, 21, 19, 17, 15, 13, 11, 9, 7, 5, 3, 1

18-st repeat

*See Notes for Row 31.

end
35" left front
35" back
47" right front
49" body
53" left & right front
53" back

end
35" right front
37" body
41" left & right front
41" back
43" body
47" left front
47" back

beg
35" left front
37" body
41" left & right front
41" back
43" body
47" back
47" right front

beg
35" back
35" right front
47" left front
49" body
53" left & right front
53" back

---

center of underarm CO sts, then pick up and knit 6 (8, 13, 15, 10, 11, 15) sts along first half of CO sts, M1 (see Glossary) in corner between CO sts and held sts, work 73 (75, 77, 73, 83, 85, 87) held sleeve sts as established, M1 in corner between sleeve sts and CO sts, pick up and knit 7 (9, 14, 16, 11, 12, 16) sts along other half of CO sts—88 (94, 106, 106, 106, 110, 120) sts total. Pm and join for working in rnds.

NEXT RND: K5 (7, 12, 14, 9, 10, 14), k2tog, work in patt to last 8 (10, 15, 17, 12, 13, 17) sts, k2tog, k6 (8, 13, 15, 10, 11, 15)—86 (92, 104, 104, 104, 108, 118) sts rem.

Work 1 rnd even in patt, working sts outside chart section in St st.

DEC RND: K2, k2tog, work in patt to last 4 sts, ssk, k2—2 sts dec'd.

Cont in patt, rep the dec rnd every other rnd 0 (0, 0, 4, 4, 6) more times, then every 4th rnd 9 (9, 14, 14, 10, 12, 11) times, then every 6th rnd 3 (3, 0, 0, 0, 0, 0) times, changing to dpn in larger size when sts no longer fit comfortably on cir needle—60 (66, 74, 74, 74, 74, 82) sts rem.

Work even in patt until sleeve measures about 11" (28 cm) from dividing row for all sizes, ending with Rnd 6 of Sleeve chart.

Cuff

Knit 6 rnds, purl 1 rnd for hem fold line—sleeve measures about 11¾"

(30 cm) from dividing rnd. Change to smaller dpn and knit 6 more rnds for facing.

BO all sts.

Fold facing to WS along fold line and, with yarn threaded on a tapestry needle, whipstitch (see Glossary) in place.

Finishing

Block pieces to measurements.

Neckband

With longer cir needle in larger size and RS facing, pick up and knit 140 (140, 140, 140, 172, 172, 172) sts evenly spaced around neck opening. Do not join. Beg and ending

Make It Yours

Stitch pattern breakdown:

MAIN BODY: Multiple of 18 stitches plus 1 balancing stitch.

SIDE INSERT: 11-stitch panel.

Choose any pattern with a multiple of 18 stitches plus 1 to substitute for the chandelier lace pattern used here. You can also use a pattern with a multiple of 9 stitches plus 1, repeating the 9-stitch pattern twice for every 18-stitch repeat in the original.

For an even better custom fit, substitute a wider or narrower lace panel for the 11-stitch side insert used here.

with a WS row, work in k2, p2 rib until piece measures 1" (2.5 cm) from pick-up row.

With RS facing, BO all sts in patt.

Buttonband

With longer cir needle in larger size and RS facing, pick up and knit 120 (120, 120, 124, 128, 128, 132) sts evenly spaced along left front edge. Beg and ending with a WS row, work 5 rows in k2, p2 rib. With RS facing, BO all sts in patt.

Buttonhole Band

Mark placement of 9 buttonholes on right front, one ½" (1.3 cm) up from lower edge, one ½" (1.3 cm) down from neck edge, and the others evenly spaced in between. With longer cir needle in larger size and RS facing, pick up and knit 120 (120, 120, 124, 128, 128, 132) sts evenly spaced along right front edge. Work 2 rows in k2, p2 rib, ending with a RS row.

BUTTONHOLE ROW: (WS) Cont in patt, use the one-row method (see Glossary), to make a 2-st buttonhole opposite each marked buttonhole position.

Work in patt for 2 more rows, ending with a WS row.

With RS facing, BO all sts in patt.

Weave in loose ends. Block again, if desired. Sew buttons to buttonband, opposite buttonholes.

Left Front—sizes 35", 37", 41", 43"

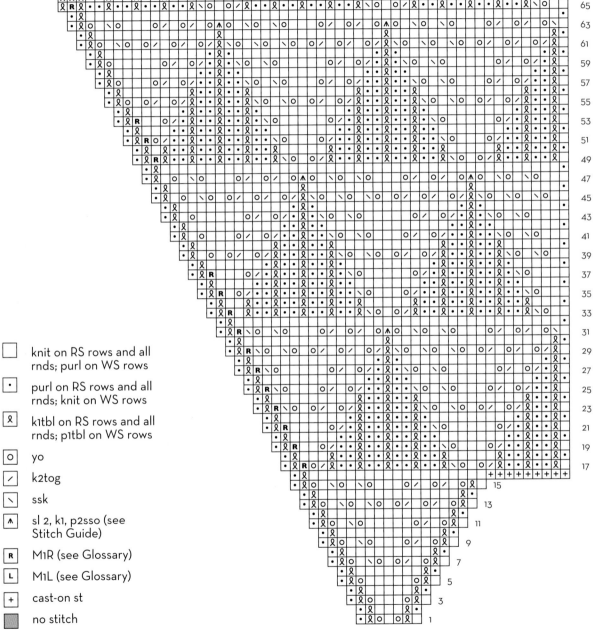

knit on RS rows and all rnds; purl on WS rows

· purl on RS rows and all rnds; knit on WS rows

ℛ k1tbl on RS rows and all rnds; p1tbl on WS rows

O yo

╱ k2tog

╲ ssk

Λ sl 2, k1, p2sso (see Stitch Guide)

R M1R (see Glossary)

L M1L (see Glossary)

+ cast-on st

▨ no stitch

▢ pattern repeat

Left Front—sizes 47", 49", 53"

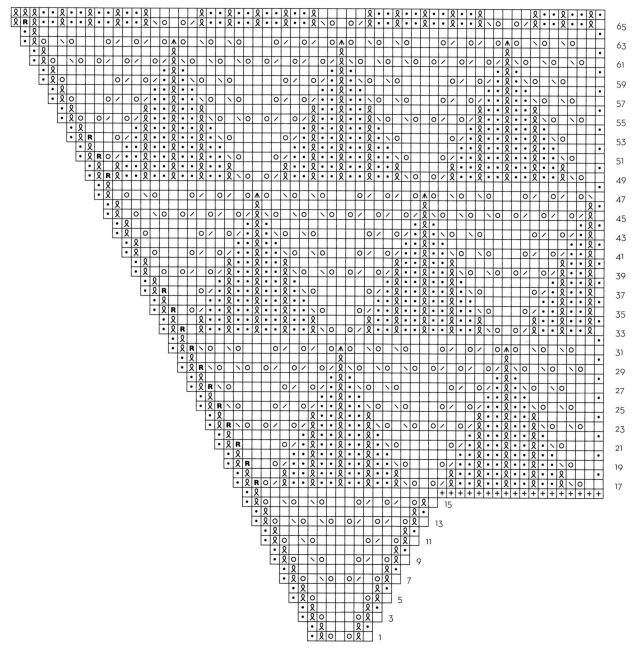

Right Front—sizes 47", 49", 53"

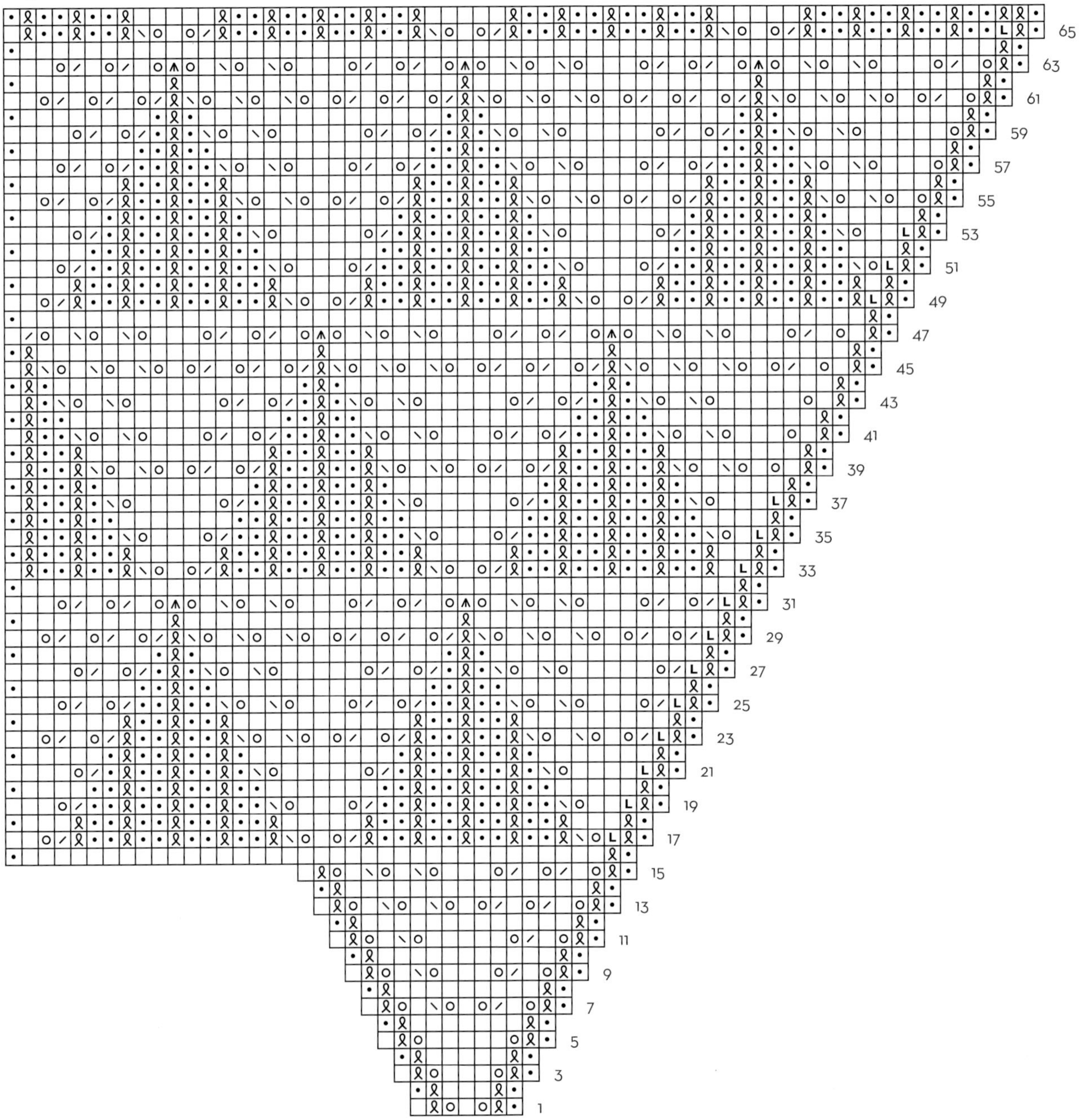

Right Front—sizes 35", 37", 41", 43"

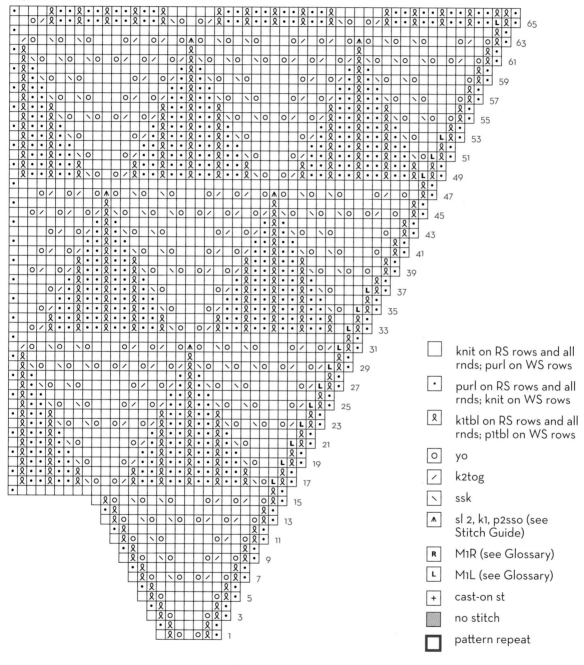

knit on RS rows and all rnds; purl on WS rows

· purl on RS rows and all rnds; knit on WS rows

Ⴒ k1tbl on RS rows and all rnds; p1tbl on WS rows

O yo

∕ k2tog

∖ ssk

Λ sl 2, k1, p2sso (see Stitch Guide)

R M1R (see Glossary)

L M1L (see Glossary)

+ cast-on st

no stitch

pattern repeat

Shaping Lace Garments

by **Eunny Jang**

Adapted from "Beyond the Basics," *Interweave Knits*, Fall 2006

Knitting lace patterns by hand is a satisfying exercise in a world that often moves too fast. The knitting is rhythmic and meditative; the finished project is a tangible expression of tradition and history. In her primer on knitted lace (see page 6), Jackie Erickson-Schweitzer discusses the basics of knitted lace: how yarnovers and decreases are paired to create lace patterns, how to read lace charts, and how to fix mistakes. Shaping a garment instead of a lace motif uses a different but complementary process.

SHAPING LACE PROJECTS

Many lace projects—shawls, stoles, and scarves—require minimal shaping, or none at all. Rectangular scarves and stoles, for example, are knitted straight up from the cast-on edge. After the lace pattern is established, it repeats without interruption. In circular shawls worked from the center out, increases are worked into the pattern repeats, and triangular shawls often use columns of yarnovers (without accompanying decreases) along a center spine and/or along the edges for shaping. In these projects, the basic repeat of the lace pattern remains intact as you knit, and the charts and written instructions spell out where to place the increased stitches and how to work them.

Garments of lace, however, are often shaped with increases and decreases along side seams and bind-offs at armholes. Shaping often cuts into pattern repeats, wreaking havoc with the balance of yarnovers and decreases. Remember that in lace pattern repeats, the number of stitches increased through yarnovers is usually balanced by the number of stitches decreased to maintain a constant stitch count. Adding or removing stitches for shaping purposes interferes with that balance unless the knitter understands the yarnover/decrease structure in the pattern repeat and takes time to plan ahead.

Two methods for shaping will allow you to add and subtract stitches at the edges of your piece while maintaining the correct number of stitches overall. The simplest method is to work any edge stitches that fall before and after the first and last full repeats of the pattern in a plain stitch that matches the background of the lace fabric—usually stockinette stitch. The second, less conspicuous, way to shape lace is to continue the pattern right up to the edge by working partial repeats on either side of the first and last full repeats. Either way, becoming thoroughly familiar with the pattern, anticipating the stitch count on every row, and using a visual guide can all be helpful.

USING A CHART TO PLAN FOR SHAPING

Patterns that provide charts often indicate shaping lines on the grid, but written instructions may not give any clue beyond, "Work X repeats of lace pattern, decreasing 1 stitch at each edge every 4th row 3 times and then increasing 1 stitch at each edge every 2nd row 6 times." Charting the lace pattern and drawing the decreases and increases as they occur will help you to keep the stitch count consistent. On graph paper, chart two or three pattern repeats beginning with the first row of the work, as shown in **Figure 1**. (You don't need to chart the entire width of your knitting, only enough repeats at either edge to accommodate the number of stitches added or removed by the shaping.) Then draw a line to indicate the shaping and another vertical line to show the beginning of the first full repeat and the end of the last full repeat. In **Figure 1**, the heavy black line shows the right edge of the knitted piece and a series of decreases worked every four rows, beginning with Row 1. The dotted line indicates the beginning of the first full repeat.

After mapping your lace pattern and adding the marker and shaping lines, compare it to the knitting on your needle. From the right side of the work, divide your stitches in the following way: place two stitch markers, one at the beginning of the first full pattern repeat and one at the end of the last full repeat. If the row begins and ends with a full repeat, place the marker one repeat in (in this example, six stitches) from either edge. You'll have three sections: the shaped right edge of the piece to the right of the first marker, the straight middle of uninterrupted pattern repeats, and the shaped left edge of the piece, to the left of the second marker.

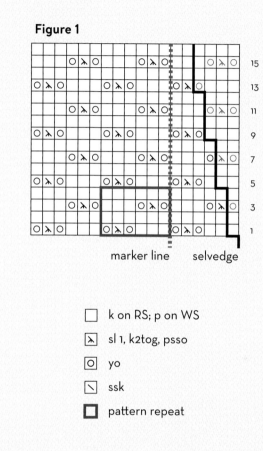

Figure 1

marker line   selvedge

☐ k on RS; p on WS

⅄ sl 1, k2tog, psso

○ yo

╲ ssk

▣ pattern repeat

SHAPING WITH DECREASES
Decreasing Stitches in Stockinette Stitch

The simplest way to work decreases in a lace piece is to switch from the lace pattern to plain stitches (usually stockinette) in the areas before and after the markers as soon as it is no longer possible to work a full pattern repeat. Allover-patterned garments (and some triangular shawls) are often shaped this way. The gauge difference between the solid and openwork sections is usually negligible after blocking. However, if the body pattern is very open and airy, a distinct "stair step" effect will be visible where solid fabric and lace meet.

Whenever the number of stitches between marker and edge is fewer than the number required for the full repeat—in

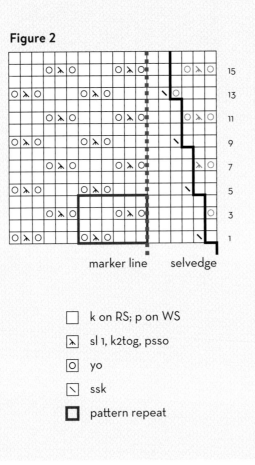

Figure 2

15

13

11

9

7

5

3

1

marker line   selvedge

□ k on RS; p on WS

⅄ sl 1, k2tog, psso

○ yo

＼ ssk

■ pattern repeat

Decreasing Stitches in Pattern

If you don't want to interrupt the flow of the lace pattern by working plain stitches at the edges, you can work with partial repeats in a way that maintains the necessary stitch count while keeping the integrity of the pattern. Once you've charted your pattern and have marked off the stitches on your needle to correspond with the sections on the chart as previously explained, focus on the number of stitches between the marker and the edge (the incomplete pattern repeat), noting the relationship of those stitches to the row below, and to the whole repeat. Remember that yarnovers make a new stitch without affecting any stitches from the row below, while decreases reduce two or three stitches from the row below into a single stitch.

According to the chart of the original pattern in **Figure 1**, there should be five stitches between the marker and edge on Row 3 after working the first decrease in Row 1. Take a look at the work on the needle and imagine each stitch you'll make, going from the marker out to the edge. Following the chart in **Figure 1**, you can see three plain stitches immediately precede the marker, then a yarnover, and then a double decrease (which eliminates two stitches) to begin the row. If you make a double decrease over the first three stitches and then work a yarnover, you will be left with only four stitches before the marker instead of five, and the pattern will be off by one stitch.

this example, the repeat requires six stitches—simply ignore lace patterning and knit the stitches plain, incorporating any shaping at the extreme edges of the piece. In **Figure 2**, Row 1 shows the first decrease. (Remember that each square on the chart represents one stitch after the row has been completed.) Work the first six stitches as ssk, k4, work the center section in pattern, and work the last six stitches of the row outside the second marker as k4, k2tog (not shown on the chart)—five stitches remain between each marker and the selvedge. On Rows 2–4 work the five stitches at each side in stockinette as shown in **Figure 2**.

If, eventually, all the stitches between marker and edge have been eliminated, and there are still decreases to be made, simply reposition the markers at the beginning and end of the first and last full repeats and continue in the same manner.

Think of how pattern elements work together in the whole repeat: the double decrease represents an action happening to three stitches from the row below, the stitch to the right of the decrease symbol (which has already been decreased away), the stitch directly below it, and the stitch to the left of it. In order to keep the stitch count correct, the actual work needs to turn two, not three, stitches into one. **Figure 3** shows how to work a partial repeat of the pattern in a way that maintains the stitch count. In Row 3, the symbol at the beginning of the row has changed to show a single (ssk) decrease. Count this decrease as the first stitch of the row. Then work yo, k3 to the marker. When you finish the row, five stitches will remain between the marker and the edge.

In **Figures 1 and 3**, the chart shows a shaping decrease at the beginning of Row 5. Work the first two stitches together as ssk and continue in pattern.

According to the original pattern (**Figure 1**), Row 7 would begin with a yarnover as the first of four stitches between marker and edge. Consider again what the whole pattern repeat looks like—a double decrease and another yarnover originally preceded the remaining yarnover in Row 7. A single yarnover without an accompanying decrease is unbalanced—if worked, it would create a new stitch and increase the stitch count by one. The solution? Simply ignore the yarnover and knit the first stitch of the row to maintain

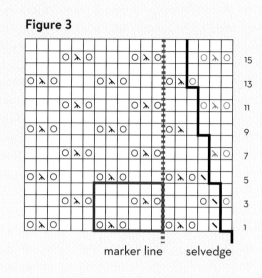

Figure 3

marker line   selvedge

the right number of stitches between marker and edge.

In Rows 9 and 13, each double decrease removes two stitches, and the single yarnover restores one of those two stitches, resulting in a decrease of one stitch. Because both Rows 9 and 13 are decrease rows, simply omitting the yarnover in front of each double decrease, as shown in **Figure 3**, will reduce the stitch count by one stitch as the shaping requires.

SHAPING WITH INCREASES
Increasing Stitches in Stockinette Stitch

Stockinette stitch can also be used to work increases along the edge of a sweater body or sleeve. Place markers before and after the first

and last full repeats as explained before, and work the stitches between the marker and the edge in stockinette stitch, increasing when shown on the chart and using the increase technique called for in the pattern. If no particular increase technique is spelled out, you can cast on a new stitch at the edge using the backward-loop cast-on (see Glossary), or work a make 1 (M1) or raised bar increase (see Glossary) one stitch in from the edge. When enough stitches have been added to work an entire repeat, move the marker to the outside of the new repeat and work the newly introduced edge stitches according to the row of the pattern you're on. (You don't need to wait until Row 1 of the pattern to start working the pattern over the new stitches.)

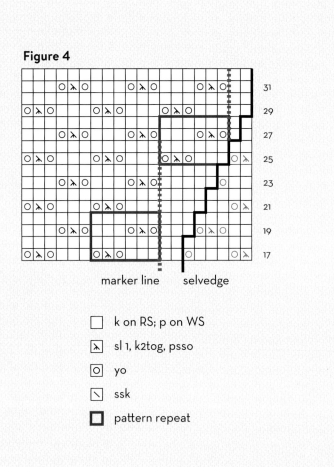

Figure 4

			O	⋏	O			O	⋏	O			O	⋏	O			31
O	⋏	O			O	⋏	O			O	⋏	O						29
		O	⋏	O			O	⋏	O			O	⋏	O				27
O	⋏	O			O	⋏	O			O	⋏	O		O	⋏		25
		O	⋏	O			O	⋏	O			O			O			23
O	⋏	O			O	⋏	O			O	⋏	O	O	⋏		21
		O	⋏	O			O	⋏	O		O	⋏	O				19
O	⋏	O			O	⋏	O		O			O	⋏		17

marker line   selvedge

- ☐ k on RS; p on WS
- ⋏ sl 1, k2tog, psso
- O yo
- ◣ ssk
- ▣ pattern repeat

In the example in **Figure 4**, one stitch is increased every right-side row, beginning with Row 19. When Row 25 has been completed, there are six stitches between the marker and edge—enough stitches to work a full repeat if you are increasing by casting on a new stitch at the end of the needle. If you are working an increase one stitch in from the selvedge, you'll need to wait until you have seven stitches between marker and selvedge to begin a new repeat. On the next lace pattern row (Row 27 in this example), move the marker to the outside of the new six-stitch repeat and work stockinette between the new marked position and the selvedge as before.

Increasing Stitches in Pattern

You increase stitches in pattern in much the same way that you decrease them.

Plot the pattern, marker, and shaping lines, and first and last full repeats on a chart, as shown in **Figure 5** (the figure shows only the first full repeat). Place markers on your needle before and after the first and last full pattern repeats. Again, focus on the number of stitches between marker and edge and remember that each square on the chart equals one stitch on the needle after the row is completed. In Row 17 of this example, there are two stitches before the first marker. Count stitches from the marker to the edge to decide how to handle the partial repeat. Here, instead of working a double decrease and yarnover as shown in **Figure 5**, work a single decrease to balance the single yarnover and maintain the stitch count of two as shown in **Figure 6**. Row 19 is the first increase row, and you can simply increase one stitch to bring the stitch count before the marker to three as shown.

In Row 21, the three stitches of the preceding row need to become four stitches worked, according to the chart and counting back from the marker, as a yarnover, a double decrease, a yarnover, and a plain stitch (the increased stitch). The yarnovers create a whole new stitch without affecting any from the row below, but the double decrease will reduce all three available stitches of Row 20 into one stitch, leaving nothing to increase from. To solve the problem, cast on one stitch at the edge with a knitted or backward-loop cast-on, knit that stitch as the first stitch of the row, and continue.

In Row 23, the four stitches of the preceding row must become five, but the row as shown in the original chart (**Figure 5**) starts with the same unbalanced partial repeat that appeared at the beginning of Row 17. Again, count from the marker—three plain stitches precede it, then a yarnover, then a double decrease. Using the principles learned when decreasing, think about how the previous row's stitches will be used in this row—three available stitches can be used for the three plain stitches of Row 23, and the yarnover doesn't require a stitch from the previous row, leaving one stitch for the square containing the double decrease symbol. Of course, working a double decrease would throw everything off by two stitches. Solution? Work the first stitch plain, work the yarnover required by the pattern without any companion decrease at all to increase to five stitches between the marker and the selvedge, as shown in **Figure 6**, and continue.

After Row 25, there are six stitches between marker and edge, enough to work a full repeat. On the next lace patterned row, Row 27, move the marker to set off those six stitches as the new first full repeat, and continue.

As you grow more familiar with how lace works, markers will take a back seat to your own ability to read the work and intuitively know what needs to be done. If you understand how the unglamorous building blocks of knitted lace—yarnovers and decreases—work together, then you'll be able to master shaping in the most complex constructions and patterns.

Figure 5

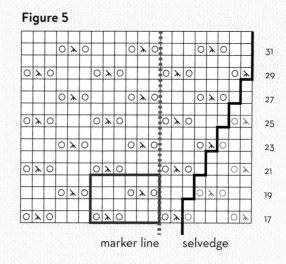

marker line   selvedge

Figure 6

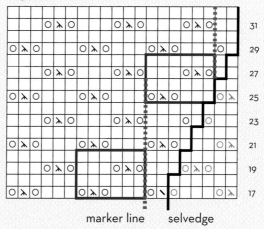

marker line   selvedge

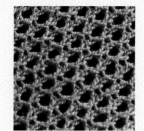

Hotel Tassel
wrap

by **Åsa Tricosa**

Wearing Åsa Tricosa's stunning lace and cables wrap is like wrapping yourself in a work of fine art. Molding the yarn into an Art Nouveau–inspired mix of lace mesh, garter edge detail, and with a cabled motif that runs its whole length, this wrap shows as much thought in every stitch as Victor Horta put into the masterpiece that inspired the piece, Hotel Tassel.

Finished Size

About 19" (48.5 cm) wide and 58" (147.5 cm) long.

Yarn

Laceweight (#0 Lace).

SHOWN HERE: Miss Babs Yet (65% merino, 35% tussah silk; 400 yd [366 m]/65 g): moss, 2 skeins.

Needles

WRAP: Size U.S. 4 (3.5 mm): 32" (80 cm) circular (cir).

CAST-ON: Size U.S. 3 (3.25 mm): 32" (80 cm) cir.

Adjust needle sizes if necessary to obtain the correct gauge.

Notions

2 cable needles (cn); stitch holder or waste yarn; tapestry needle.

Gauge

19 sts and 32 rows = 4" (10 cm) in Mesh pattern with larger needle.

Note

• *When working only part of the sts on a cn, work the sts on the right on the cn and keep the st(s) on the left on the cn to be worked later.*

STITCH GUIDE

Mesh Pattern

(multiple of 3 sts + 2)

(Note: This pattern as written here is only used for the gauge swatch. This patt is incorporated into Charts A and B.)

ROW 1: (RS) K1, *k2tog, yo, k1; rep from * to last st, k1.

ROWS 2 AND 4: (WS) Purl.

ROW 3: K2, *k2tog, yo, k1; rep from *.

ROW 5: K1, *yo, k1, k2tog; rep from * to last st, k1.

ROW 6: Purl.

Rep Rows 1–6 for patt.

Attached I-Cord Edging

Use the cable method (see Glossary) to CO 3 sts, k4, *sl 4 sts from right needle to left needle, k3, k2togtbl; rep from * until 4 sts rem on right needle, sl 4 sts from right needle to left needle, sl 1, BO 1, k2togtbl, pass slipped st over—1 st rem. Fasten off.

Wrap

With smaller cir needle, use the Turkish method (see Glossary) to CO 109 sts. Change to larger needle.

SET-UP ROW: (WS) Sl 1 pwise wyf, k1, sl 1 pwise wyf, purl to last 3 sts, sl 1 pwise wyf, k1, sl 1 pwise wyf. Sl sts from provisional CO onto st holder or waste yarn.

Work Rows 1–100 of Chart A— 103 sts rem.

Work Rows 101–106 forty-five times.

Work Rows 1–98 of Chart B— 109 sts.

BO using the attached I-cord edging (see Stitch Guide).

Finishing

Carefully remove waste yarn from provisional CO and return 109 sts to larger cir needle. BO using the attached I-cord edging.

Weave in loose ends. Block to measurements.

Mesh

(used for gauge swatch only)

☐ knit on RS; purl on WS

☑ yo

☑ k2tog

☐ pattern repeat

Get Inspired

Designed by the famous Art Nouveau architect Victor Horta, Belgium's Hotel Tassel is one of the most recognized buildings from that era. The structure consists of two main buildings built with brick and stone, joined together by a third glass-covered steel building, bringing light into the center. This building is unique because each element was designed by Horta himself, from the doorknobs, to the staircases, to the mosaic-covered flooring, to the wall panels down to the windows.

Chart A

	knit on RS; purl on WS		R	M1R
	purl on RS; knit on WS		L	M1L
	yo		P	M1P
	k2tog		$+$	kfb
	ssk			pattern repeat
	sl 1 pwise wyf on RS			sl 1 st onto cn and hold in front, k1, k1 from cn
	sl 1 pwise wyf on WS			sl 1 st onto cn and hold in back, k1, k1 from cn
	s2kp			sl 3 sts onto cn and hold in front, k1; k1, sl 1 pwise wyf, k1 from cn
	no stitch			

Chart B

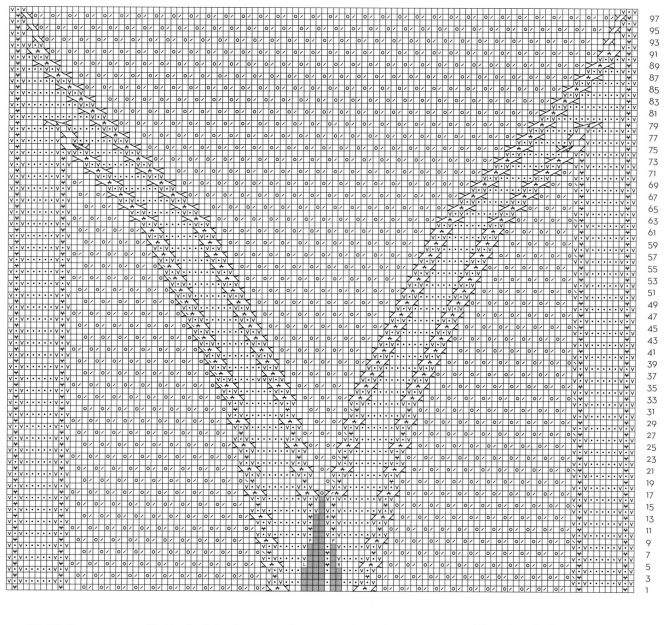

97
95
93
91
89
87
85
83
81
79
77
75
73
71
69
67
65
63
61
59
57
55
53
51
49
47
45
43
41
39
37
35
33
31
29
27
25
23
21
19
17
15
13
11
9
7
5
3
1

sl 1 st onto cn and hold in back, k1, sl 1 pwise wyf, k1; k1 from cn

sl 2 sts onto cn and hold in back, k1, sl 1 pwise wyf, k1; k2 from cn

sl 3 sts onto cn and hold in front, k2; k1, sl 1 pwise wyf, k1 from cn

sl 2 sts onto cn and hold in front, k1; k2 from cn

sl 1 st onto cn and hold in back, k2; k1 from cn

sl 3 sts onto cn and hold in front, k1 from left needle; k2 from cn; k1 from left needle; k1 from cn

sl 2 sts onto cn and hold in back, k1 from left needle; k1 from cn; k2 from left needle; k1 from cn

sl 3 sts onto cn and hold in front, k1; k1, sl 1 pwise wyf from cn, ssk last st of cn with next st on left needle

sl 1 st onto cn and hold in back, k2 from left needle, sl 1 st onto second cn and hold in back, k1 from left needle, k1 from first cn, k1 from second cn

sl 1 st onto cn and hold in front, k1 from left needle, sl 2 sts onto second cn and hold in front, k1 from left needle, k1 from first cn, k2 from second cn

sl 3 sts onto cn and hold in front, [kfb] 2 times, sk2p from cn

sl 2 sts onto cn and hold in back, k3tog, [kfb] 2 times from cn

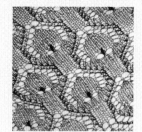

Fountain Pen
shawl

by **Susan Pierce Lawrence**

Lace goes literary in this exquisite triangular shawl, which features a motif in the shape of a classic fountain pen nib. Curving lozenges punctuated with eyelets and nupps—bobble-like clusters of stitches—give the pattern its dimensions. After trying several edging variations, Susan Pierce Lawrence settled on a simple pattern that accents but doesn't compete with the strong curving line of the basic design.

Finished Size
78" (198 cm) wide at top edge and 39" (99 cm) long, measured down centerline, after blocking.

Yarn
Laceweight (#0 Lace).

SHOWN HERE: Lorna's Laces Helen's Lace (50% silk, 50% wool; 1,250 yd [1143 m]/113 g): #9NS pewter, 1 skein.

Needles
Size 6 (4 mm): straight or 24" (60 cm) circular (cir).

Adjust needle size if necessary to obtain the correct gauge.

Notions
Coil-less safety pin; tapestry needle; T-pins for blocking.

Gauge
16 sts and 24 rows = 4" (10 cm) in St st, after blocking.

Notes

- *This shawl is worked from the center back of the neck down to the bottom edge. The main body of the shawl is worked first, followed by the bottom border. The triangular shape is created by working yarnover increases on the inside of the garter-stitch borders and on each side of the center stitch. These increases are worked on right-side rows only. Use a coil-less safety pin to mark the center stitch. No other markers are necessary, although you may choose to place one before and after the 2-stitch garter borders. If using additional markers, remove them before working Border chart. To minimize errors, it is helpful to count your stitches as you work each wrong-side row. The stitch count increases by 4 stitches each time you complete a right-side row, there is always an odd number of stitches on each side of the center stitch, and the total stitch count is always an odd number.*

- *Because the bottom border flows directly from the main stitch pattern, the shawl can easily be made larger or smaller by working more or fewer repeats of the Body chart before beginning the Border chart. The sample shawl used about 77 grams (2.7 ounces) of the recommended yarn. Increasing the size of the shawl will require more yarn.*

STITCH GUIDE

Nupp

(K1, yo, k1, yo, k1) in same st.

Shawl

Using the knitted method (see Glossary), CO 5 sts.

Set up patt:

ROWS 1 AND 2: Knit.

ROW 3: K2, yo, k1 (center st), yo, k2—7 sts.

Mark center st using coil-less safety pin and move up work as needed.

ROW 4: K2, p3, k2.

Body

Work Rows 1–20 of Lace Beginning chart once—47 sts. Work Rows 1–16 of Body chart 10 times—367 sts.

Lower Border

Work Rows 1–24 of Border chart once—415 sts.

Bind Off

note: *This two-step BO ensures a stretchy bottom edge that blocks easily. Work Row 2 loosely.*

ROW 1: (RS) K2, yo, k14, [yo, k1, yo, k15] 11 times, yo, k1, yo, k14, yo, k1 (center st), yo, k14, [yo, k1, yo, k15] 11 times, yo, k1, yo, k14, yo, k2—467 sts.

ROW 2: K1, *k1, insert tip of left needle into the front of the 2 sts on the right needle and knit them tog; rep from * until all sts are BO.

Finishing

Weave in loose ends but do not trim. Soak shawl in cool water until thoroughly wet. Gently squeeze out the excess water, then place the shawl between two towels and press firmly to remove additional water. Block by pinning the damp shawl to a flat surface, pulling the points out along the bottom edge. Do not remove the pins until the shawl is completely dry. Trim yarn ends.

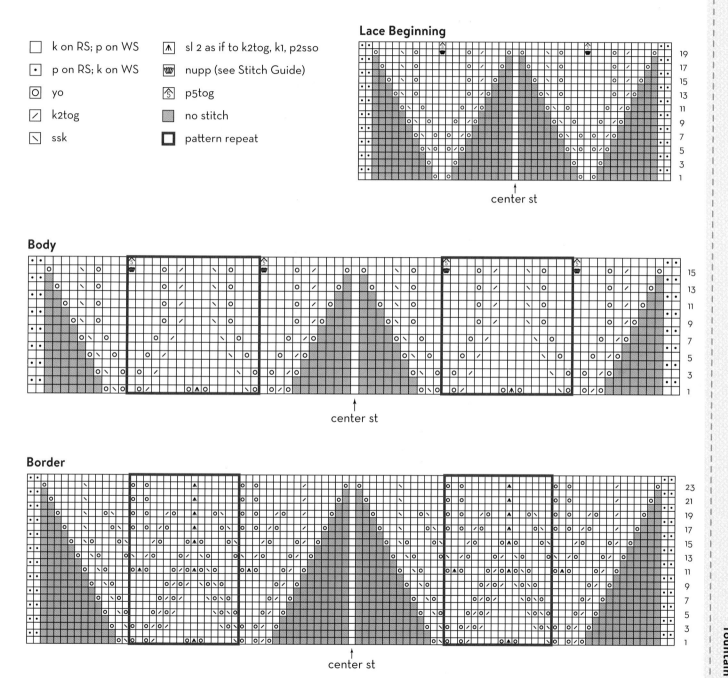

Legend

- ☐ k on RS; p on WS
- ⦁ p on RS; k on WS
- ⦾ yo
- ⟋ k2tog
- ⟍ ssk
- ⚠ sl 2 as if to k2tog, k1, p2sso
- nupp (see Stitch Guide)
- p5tog
- no stitch
- ☐ pattern repeat

Lace Beginning

center st

Body

center st

Border

center st

Brooklyn Bridge
cardigan

by **Melissa Wehrle**; photos by **Heather Weston**

The addition of a triple leaf lace border takes a simple open cardigan and makes it a welcome addition to any wardrobe. The lace continues around the hood, adding a feminine touch to an otherwise sporty detail. The fingering-weight wool feels light but gives just enough warmth for chilly air-conditioned offices, a walk through the city at night, or even a breezy afternoon at Brooklyn Bridge Park.

Finished Size
32 (35, 37½, 40½, 44, 48, 52)" (81.5 [89, 95, 103, 112, 122, 132] cm) bust circumference with fronts meeting at center. Cardigan shown measures 32" (81.5 cm).

Yarn
Fingering weight (#1 Super Fine).

SHOWN HERE: Lorna's Laces Shepherd Sock (80% superwash merino wool, 20% nylon; 430 yd [393 m]/100 g): poppy, 4 (5, 5, 5, 6, 6, 6) skeins.

Needles
BODY AND SLEEVES: Size U.S. 4 (3.5 mm): 24" (61 cm) circular (cir).

Adjust needle size if necessary to obtain the correct gauge.

Notions
Markers (m); stitch holders; tapestry needle.

Gauge
27 sts and 34 rows = 4" (10 cm) in St st.

15 to 19 sts of Triple Leaf chart (see Notes) measure 2¼" (5.5 cm) wide.

3-stitch I-cord edgings measure about ¼" (6 mm) wide each.

Notes

- I-cord edging makes a nice clean finish along the front edges and hood of this cardigan. In this project, it is especially helpful for two reasons. First, it eliminates the extra finishing step of picking up and working front band stitches. Second, when the hood is folded back there is no visible pick-up ridge to ruin the clean look of the cardigan.

- The stitch count of the Triple Leaf chart does not remain constant throughout. It begins with 15 stitches in Rows 1–4, increases to 17 stitches in Rows 5 and 6, then increases again to 19 stitches in Rows 7 and 8, then decreases back to 15 stitches again for Rows 11 and 12. Always count the stitches of each panel as 15 stitches, even if the pattern is on a row where the stitch count has temporarily increased.

STITCH GUIDE

I-cord Edging
(worked over 3 edge sts)

RIGHT FRONT: On RS rows, work first 3 sts as k3; and on WS rows, work the last 3 sts as sl 3 purlwise with yarn in front (pwise wyf).

LEFT FRONT: On RS rows, work the last 3 sts as sl 3 as if to purl with yarn in back (pwise wyb); and on WS rows, work the first 3 sts as p3.

Back

CO 116 (126, 134, 144, 158, 176, 190) sts. Beg with a WS row, work 8 rows in St st, ending with a RS row. Knit 1 WS row for hem fold line. Work in St st until piece measures 4" (10 cm) from fold line, ending with a WS row.

Shape Waist

DEC ROW: (RS) K1, ssk (see Glossary), knit to last 3 sts, k2tog, k1—2 sts dec'd.

Cont in St st, rep the dec row every 6 (6, 6, 6, 6, 4, 4) rows 4 (4, 3, 3, 3, 1, 1) more time(s), then every 8 (8, 8, 8, 8, 6, 6) rows 6 (6, 7, 7, 7, 12, 12) times—94 (104, 112, 122, 136, 148, 162) sts; piece measures about 12½ (12½, 12¾, 12¾, 12¾, 13, 13)" (31.5 [31.5, 32.5, 32.5, 32.5, 33,

33] cm) from fold line. Work even for 11 rows, beg and ending with a WS row.

INC ROW: (RS) K1, M1 (see Glossary), work to last st, M1, k1—2 sts inc'd.

Cont in St st, rep the inc row every 6 (6, 6, 6, 8, 8, 8) rows 4 (4, 3, 3, 2, 6, 6) more times, then every 8 (8, 8, 8, 10, 0, 0) rows 2 (2, 3, 3, 3, 0, 0) times, working new sts in St st—108 (118, 126, 136, 148, 162, 176) sts. Work even in St st until piece measures 19½ (19½, 20, 20, 20½, 21, 21)" (49.5 [49.5, 51, 51, 52, 53.5, 53.5] cm) from fold line, ending with a WS row.

Shape Armholes

BO 7 (7, 8, 9, 10, 12, 14) sts at beg of next 2 rows—94 (104, 110, 118, 128, 138, 148) sts. Dec 1 st at each side every row 5 (6, 7, 9, 10, 12, 15)

times—84 (92, 96, 100, 108, 114, 118) sts rem. Cont in St st until armholes measure 7¾ (7¾, 8, 8¼, 8½, 8¾, 9¼)" (19.5 [19.5, 20.5, 21, 21.5, 22, 23.5] cm), ending with a WS row.

Shape Shoulders

BO 6 (7, 8, 8, 10, 10, 11) sts at the beg of the next 4 rows, then BO 7 (8, 8, 9, 9, 10, 10) sts at the beg of the next 2 rows—46 (48, 48, 50, 50, 54, 54) center back neck sts rem. Place sts on holder.

Right Front

CO 58 (63, 67, 72, 79, 88, 95) sts. Beg with a WS row, work 8 rows in St st, ending with a RS row.

NEXT ROW: (WS) Knit to end for fold line, then use the knitted

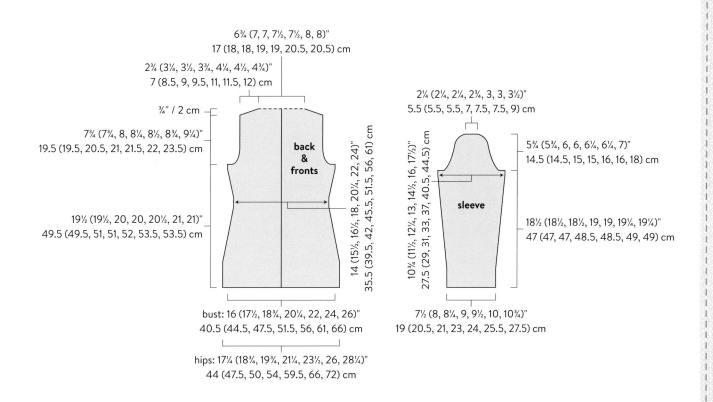

6¾ (7, 7, 7½, 7½, 8, 8)"
17 (18, 18, 19, 19, 20.5, 20.5) cm

2¾ (3¼, 3½, 3¾, 4¼, 4½, 4¾)"
7 (8.5, 9, 9.5, 11, 11.5, 12) cm

¾" / 2 cm

7¾ (7¾, 8, 8¼, 8½, 8¾, 9¼)"
19.5 (19.5, 20.5, 21, 21.5, 22, 23.5) cm

back & fronts

14 (15½, 16½, 18, 20¼, 22, 24)"
35.5 (39.5, 42, 45.5, 51.5, 56, 61) cm

19½ (19½, 20, 20, 20½, 21, 21)"
49.5 (49.5, 51, 51, 52, 53.5, 53.5) cm

bust: 16 (17½, 18¾, 20¼, 22, 24, 26)"
40.5 (44.5, 47.5, 51.5, 56, 61, 66) cm

hips: 17¼ (18¾, 19¾, 21¼, 23½, 26, 28¼)"
44 (47.5, 50, 54, 59.5, 66, 72) cm

2¼ (2¼, 2¼, 2¾, 3, 3, 3½)"
5.5 (5.5, 5.5, 7, 7.5, 7.5, 9) cm

5¾ (5¾, 6, 6, 6¼, 6¼, 7)"
14.5 (14.5, 15, 15, 16, 16, 18) cm

sleeve

10¾ (11¼, 12¼, 13, 14½, 16, 17½)"
27.5 (29, 31, 33, 37, 40.5, 44.5) cm

18½ (18½, 18½, 19, 19, 19¼, 19¼)"
47 (47, 47, 48.5, 48.5, 49, 49) cm

7½ (8, 8¼, 9, 9½, 10, 10¾)"
19 (20.5, 21, 23, 24, 25.5, 27.5) cm

method (see Glossary) to CO 3 sts at end of row—61 (66, 70, 75, 82, 91, 98) sts.

Working 3 new CO sts at front edge in I-cord edging (see Stitch Guide), work 8 rows in St st, ending with a WS row.

NEXT ROW: (RS) Work 3 edging sts as established, k3, place marker (pm), work Row 1 of Triple Leaf chart over 15 sts, pm, knit to end.

Working patts as established, work even until piece measures 4" (10 cm) from fold line, ending with a WS row.

Shape Waist

DEC ROW: (RS) Work in patt to last 3 sts, k2tog, k1—1 st dec'd.

Cont in patt, rep the dec row every 6 (6, 6, 6, 6, 4, 4) rows 4 (4, 3, 3, 3, 1, 1) more time(s), then every 8 (8, 8, 8, 8, 6, 6) rows 6 (6, 7, 7, 7, 12, 12) times—50 (55, 59, 64, 71, 77,

84) sts (see Notes about counting chart sts); piece measures about 12½ (12½, 12¾, 12¾, 12¾, 13, 13)" (31.5 [31.5, 32.5, 32.5, 32.5, 33, 33] cm) from fold line. Work even for 11 rows, beg and ending with a WS row.

INC ROW: (RS) Work in patt to last st, M1, k1—1 st inc'd.

Cont in patt, rep the inc row every 6 (6, 6, 6, 8, 8, 8) rows 4 (4, 3, 3, 2, 6, 6) more times, then every 8 (8, 8, 8, 10, 0, 0) rows 2 (2, 3, 3, 3, 0, 0) times, working new sts in St st—57 (62, 66, 71, 77, 84, 91) sts. Work even in patt until piece measures 19½ (19½, 20, 20, 20½, 21, 21)" (49.5 [49.5, 51, 51, 52, 53.5, 53.5] cm) from fold line, ending with a RS row.

Shape Armhole

BO 7 (7, 8, 9, 10, 12, 14) sts at beg of next WS row—50 (55, 58, 62, 67, 72, 77) sts. Dec 1 st at armhole edge (end of RS rows, beg of WS

rows) every row 5 (6, 7, 9, 10, 12, 15) times—45 (49, 51, 53, 57, 60, 62) sts rem. Cont in patt until armholes measure 7¾ (7¾, 8, 8¼, 8½, 8¾, 9¼)" (19.5 [19.5, 20.5, 21, 21.5, 22, 23.5] cm), ending with a RS row. Make a note of the last chart row completed so you can work the left front armhole to match.

Shape Shoulder

BO 6 (7, 8, 8, 10, 10, 11) sts at the beg of the next 2 WS rows, then BO 7 (8, 8, 9, 9, 10, 10) sts at the beg of the next WS row—26 (27, 27, 28, 28, 30, 30) sts rem. Make a note of the last WS chart row completed so you can resume working the patt for the hood with the correct row. Place sts on holder.

Left Front

CO 58 (63, 67, 72, 79, 88, 95) sts. Beg with a WS row, work 8 rows in St st, ending with a RS row.

NEXT ROW: (WS) Use the knitted method to CO 3 sts at beg of row, purl across new sts, knit to end for fold line—61 (66, 70, 75, 82, 91, 98) sts.

Working 3 new CO sts at front edge in I-cord edging (see Stitch Guide), work 8 rows in St st, ending with a WS row.

NEXT ROW: (RS) Knit to last 21 sts, pm, work Row 1 of Triple Leaf chart over 15 sts, pm, k3, work 3 edging sts.

Working patts as established, work even until piece measures 4" (10 cm) from fold line, ending with a WS row.

Shape Waist

DEC ROW: (RS) K1, ssk, work in patt to end—1 st dec'd.

Cont in patt, rep the dec row every 6 (6, 6, 6, 4, 4) rows 4 (4, 3, 3, 1, 1) more time(s), then every 8 (8, 8, 8, 8, 6, 6) rows 6 (6, 7, 7, 7, 12, 12) times—50 (55, 59, 64, 71, 77, 84) sts; piece measures about 12½ (12½, 12¾, 12¾, 12¾, 13, 13)" (31.5 [31.5,

32.5, 32.5, 32.5, 33, 33] cm) from fold line. Work even for 11 rows, beg and ending with a WS row.

INC ROW: (RS) K1, M1, work in patt to end—1 st inc'd.

Cont in patt, rep the inc row every 6 (6, 6, 6, 8, 8, 8) rows 4 (4, 3, 3, 2, 6, 6) more times, then every 8 (8, 8, 8, 10, 0, 0) rows 2 (2, 3, 3, 3, 0, 0) times, working new sts in St st—57 (62, 66, 71, 77, 84, 91) sts. Work even in patt until piece measures 19½ (19½, 20, 20, 20½, 21, 21)" (49.5 [49.5, 51, 51, 52, 53.5, 53.5] cm) from fold line, ending with a WS row.

Shape Armhole

BO 7 (7, 8, 9, 10, 12, 14) sts at beg of next RS row—50 (55, 58, 62, 67, 72, 77) sts. Dec 1 st at armhole edge (beg of RS rows, end of WS rows) every row 5 (6, 7, 9, 10, 12, 15) times—45 (49, 51, 53, 57, 60, 62) sts rem. Cont in patt until armholes measure 7¾ (7¾, 8, 8¼, 8½, 8¾, 9¼)" (19.5 [19.5, 20.5, 21, 21.5, 22, 23.5] cm), ending with the WS row 1 row before the RS chart row that ended the right front armhole.

Shape Shoulder

BO 6 (7, 8, 8, 10, 10, 11) sts at the beg of the next 2 RS rows, then BO 7 (8, 8, 9, 9, 10, 10) sts at the beg of the next RS row—26 (27, 27, 28, 28, 30, 30) sts rem. Work 1 WS row even to end with the same chart row as the right front. Place sts on holder.

Sleeves

CO 50 (54, 56, 60, 64, 68, 72) sts. Beg with a WS row, work 8 rows in St st, ending with a RS row. Knit 1 WS row for hem fold line. Work in St st until piece measures 3" (7.5 cm) from fold line, ending with a WS row.

INC ROW: (RS) K1, M1, work to last st, M1, k1—2 sts inc'd.

Cont in St st, rep the inc row every 12 (10, 10, 8, 8, 6, 4) rows 8 (4, 10, 1, 16, 11, 1) more time(s), then every 14 (12, 12, 10, 0, 8, 6) rows 2 (7, 2, 12, 0, 8, 21) times, working new sts in St st—72 (78, 82, 88, 98, 108, 118) sts. Work even in St st until piece measures 18½ (18½, 18½, 19, 19, 19¼,

Triple Leaf

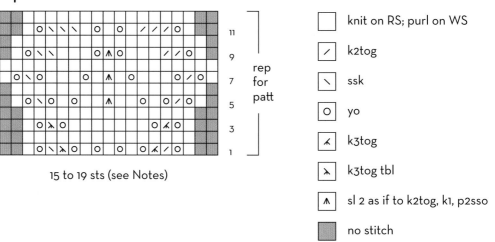

15 to 19 sts (see Notes)

	knit on RS; purl on WS
/	k2tog
\	ssk
O	yo
⅄	k3tog
λ	k3tog tbl
∧	sl 2 as if to k2tog, k1, p2sso
▓	no stitch

19¼" (47 [47, 47, 48.5, 48.5, 49, 49] cm) from fold line, ending with a WS row.

Shape Sleeve Cap

BO 7 (7, 8, 9, 10, 12, 14) sts at beg of next 2 rows—58 (64, 66, 70, 78, 84, 90) sts rem. Dec 1 st at each side every RS row 2 (3, 4, 5, 5, 6, 5) times, every 4 rows 6 (5, 6, 4, 4, 2, 5) times, every RS row 7 (6, 3, 7, 6, 8, 5) times, then every row 3 (7, 9, 7, 11, 13, 15) times—22 (22, 22, 24, 26, 26, 30) sts rem. BO 3 sts at the beg of the next 2 rows—16 (16, 16, 18, 20, 20, 24) sts. BO all sts.

Finishing

Fold lower body and sleeve hems to WS along fold lines and sew invisibly in place using yarn threaded on a tapestry needle. Block pieces to measurements.

Hood

With yarn threaded on a tapestry needle, sew shoulder seams. With RS facing, place 26 (27, 27, 28, 28, 30, 30) held right front sts on cir needle, place first 23 (24, 24, 25, 25, 27, 27) held back neck sts on needle, pm at center back, place last 23 (24, 24, 25, 25, 27, 27) back neck sts on needle, place 26 (27, 27, 28, 28, 30, 30) left front sts on needle—98 (102, 102, 106, 106, 114, 114) sts. Rejoin yarn with RS facing at right front edge. Cont in established patts, work even for 1" (2.5 cm), ending with a WS row.

INC ROW: (RS) Work in patt to 1 st before center m, M1, k1, slip marker (sl m), k1, M1, work in patt to end—2 sts inc'd.

Cont in patt, rep the inc row every 6 (6, 4, 4, 4, 6, 6) rows 6 (6, 4, 7, 5, 6, 6) more times, then every 8 (8, 6, 6, 6, 8, 8) rows 3 (3, 8, 6, 8, 4, 4) times, working new sts in St st—118

(122, 128, 134, 134, 136, 136) sts. Work 1 WS row even—hood measures about 8¼ (8¼, 8¾, 8¾, 9¼, 9¼, 9¼)" (21 [21, 22, 22, 23.5, 23.5, 23.5] cm).

NEXT ROW: (RS) Work 56 (58, 61, 64, 64, 65, 65) sts in pattern, k2tog, k1, remove center m, place rem 59 (61, 64, 67, 67, 68, 68) sts on a holder—58 (60, 63, 66, 66, 67, 67) right hood sts rem on needle.

Right Hood

NEXT ROW: (WS) Work even.

NEXT ROW: (RS) Work to last 3 sts, k2tog, k1—1 st dec'd.

Cont in patt, rep the shaping of the last 2 rows 8 more times—49 (51, 54, 57, 57, 58, 58) sts rem.

NEXT ROW: (WS) P1, p2tog, work to end—1 st dec'd.

NEXT ROW: (RS) Work to last 3 sts, k2tog, k1—1 st dec'd.

Rep the last 2 rows 5 more times, then work the WS dec row once more—36 (38, 41, 44, 44, 45, 45) sts rem; hood measures about 12 (12, 12½, 12½, 13, 13, 13)" (30.5 [30.5, 31.5, 31.5, 33, 33, 33] cm). BO all sts.

Left Hood

Return 59 (61, 64, 67, 67, 68, 68) held sts to needle and rejoin yarn with RS facing.

NEXT ROW: (RS) K1, ssk, work to end—1 st dec'd.

NEXT ROW: (WS) Work even.

Cont in patt, rep the shaping of the last 2 rows 9 more times—49 (51, 54, 57, 57, 58, 58) sts rem.

NEXT ROW: (RS) K1, ssk, work to end—1 st dec'd.

NEXT ROW: (WS) Work to last 3 sts, ssp (see Glossary), p1—1 st dec'd.

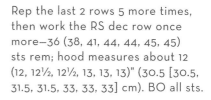

Rep the last 2 rows 5 more times, then work the RS dec row once more—36 (38, 41, 44, 44, 45, 45) sts rem; hood measures about 12 (12, 12½, 12½, 13, 13, 13)" (30.5 [30.5, 31.5, 31.5, 33, 33, 33] cm). BO all sts.

With yarn threaded on a tapestry needle, sew seam at top of hood. Sew sleeves into armholes. Sew sleeve and side seams. Weave in all loose ends. Block seams and hood, if desired.

Sea Spray
shawl

by **Angela Tong**

Easy for beginners but not sacrificing on style, Angela Tong's triangular shawlette combines an easy-to-memorize four-row lace pattern—that resembles sprays of water—with systematic yarnover increases. Worked from the bottom point up to the shoulders with the lacy border included along the way, the length can be customized by simply working fewer or more pattern repeats. Add a few garter rows at the top to prevent curling, bind off, and all that's left is weaving in the ends and blocking open the pretty lace pattern.

Finished Size

About 52" (132 cm) wide across top edge and 21½" (54.5 cm) long from top edge to bottom point, blocked.

Yarn

Fingering weight (#1 Super Fine).

SHOWN HERE: Blue Moon Fiber Arts Socks that Rock Lightweight (100% superwash merino; 405 yd [370 m]/127 g): tanzanite (purple), 2 skeins.

Needles

Size U.S. 6 (4 mm): 40" (100 cm) circular (cir).

Adjust needle size if necessary to obtain the correct gauge.

Notions

Smooth waste yarn for provisional cast-on; markers (m); tapestry needle; blocking pins.

Gauge

15 sts and 37 rows = 4" (10 cm) in 4-row stitch patt from shawl body, after blocking.

Notes

- *Each time you complete Rows 8–11 of the body section, the number of center stitches between the markers will increase by 4. For example, the first time you work Row 8 there are 9 center stitches between the markers (a multiple of 4 sts plus 1). After completing Row 9 the center section increases to 15 stitches (a multiple of 6 sts plus 3), and this count remains unchanged in Row 10. In Row 11, the center section decreases to 13 stitches—4 stitches more than the 9 center stitches in Row 8. The center 13 stitches after completing Row 11 are a multiple of 4 sts plus 5, which is equivalent to a multiple of 4 sts plus 1, so the pattern can repeat again beginning with Row 8.*

- *To adjust the finished dimensions, work more or fewer repeats of the 4-row body pattern before working the neck border. Every repeat added or removed will lengthen or shorten the distance between the top edge and bottom point by about ½" (1.3 cm) and will widen or narrow the top edge by about 1" (2.5 cm). You may need more yarn if making a larger shawl.*

STITCH GUIDE

Sl 1 pwise, k2tog, psso

Sl 1 st as if to purl (pwise), k2tog, pass slipped st over—2 sts dec'd. *Note: Slipping the first stitch pwise deliberately twists it for a decorative effect when the stitch is passed over.*

Shawl

Bottom Point

With smooth waste yarn and using a provisional method (see Glossary), CO 6 sts. Change to main yarn. Work bottom point using short-rows as foll (do not wrap any sts at the turning points):

SET-UP ROW: (WS) Knit.

ROW 1: (RS) K1, [yo, k2tog] 2 times, turn work, leaving last st unworked.

ROW 2: K5.

ROWS 3 AND 4: Knit to end.

ROWS 5 AND 6: Rep Rows 1 and 2.

ROW 7: Knit to end, do not turn.

Rotate piece 90 degrees so needle with live sts is to the right and shorter selvedge is at the top. With RS still facing, pick up and knit 1 st from garter ridge in center of selvedge. Rotate work 90 degrees again so provisional CO is at the top. Carefully remove waste yarn from provisional CO, place exposed sts on needle, and work them as k6—13 sts total.

Pattern Set-Up

SET-UP ROW: (WS) K1, yo, k2tog, k3, place marker (pm), p1, pm, k3, k2tog, yo, k1—1 center st; 6 border sts each side.

ROW 1: (RS) K2tog, k1, [yo] 2 times, k3, slip marker (sl m), yo, k1, yo, sl m, k3, [yo] 2 times, k1, k2tog—17 sts total; 3 center sts; 7 border sts each side.

ROW 2: K2tog, yo, work [k1, p1] in double yo of previous row, k2tog, k1, sl m, p3, sl m, k1, k2tog, work [p1, k1] in double yo of previous row, yo, k2tog—15 sts total; 3 center sts; 6 border sts each side.

ROW 3: K6, sl m, yo, k3, yo, sl m, k6—17 sts total; 5 center sts; 6 border sts each side.

ROW 4: K1, yo, k2tog, k3, sl m, p5, sl m, k3, k2tog, yo, k1.

ROW 5: K2tog, k1, [yo] 2 times, k3, sl m, yo, k1, yo, k3, yo, k1, yo, sl m, k3, [yo] 2 times, k1, k2tog—23 sts total; 9 center sts; 7 border sts each side.

ROW 6: K2tog, yo, work [k1, p1] in double yo of previous row, k2tog, k1, sl m, p9, sl m, k1, k2tog, work [p1, k1] in double yo of previous row, yo, k2tog—21 sts total; 9 center sts; 6 border sts each side.

ROW 7: K6, sl m, yo, k3, [sl 1 pwise, k2tog, psso (see Stitch Guide)], k3, yo, sl m, k6—still 21 sts.

Body

ROW 8: (WS) K1, yo, k2tog, k3, sl m, purl to next m, sl m, k3, k2tog, yo, k1—center sts are a multiple of 4 sts plus 1; 6 border sts each side.

ROW 9: (RS) K2tog, k1, [yo] 2 times, k3, sl m, yo, k1, *yo, k3, yo, k1; rep from * to m, yo, sl m, k3, [yo] 2 times, k1, k2tog—center sts have inc'd to a multiple of 6 sts plus 3; 7 border sts each side.

ROW 10: K2tog, yo, work [k1, p1] in double yo of previous row, k2tog, k1, sl m, purl to next m, sl m, k1, k2tog, work [p1, k1] in double yo of previous row, yo, k2tog—no change to center sts; 6 border sts each side.

ROW 11: K6, sl m, yo, *k3, sl 1 pwise, k2tog, psso; rep from * to 3 sts before next m, k3, yo, sl m, k6—center sts have dec'd to a multiple of 4 sts plus 5; 6 border sts each side; total stitch count is 4 sts more than in Row 8 (see Notes).

Rep Rows 8–11 for patt 43 more times or as desired (see Notes), ending with RS Row 11—197 sts total; 185 center sts; 6 border sts each side.

Neck Border

Knit 5 rows, beg and ending with a WS row.
BO all sts kwise.

Finishing

Weave in loose ends.

Soak in warm water for 20 minutes. Squeeze out water and roll in towels to remove excess moisture. Place on clean, flat surface and use T-pins to block to measurements. Allow to air-dry thoroughly before removing pins.

Solstice
skirt

by **Cecily Glowik MacDonald**

This shirt demonstrates an easy way to shape lace without resorting to decreases. Worked in the round from the scalloped lace pattern at the hem to the casing for the elastic at the waist, the skirt is cleverly tapered by changing to progressively smaller needles along the way, with no decreases to interrupt the lace pattern on the lower skirt.

Finished Size

About 29½ (34, 38½, 42¾, 47¼)" (75 [86.5, 98, 108.5, 120] cm) waistband circumference, 34¾ (39¼, 44, 48½, 53¼)" (88.5 [99.5, 112, 123, 135] cm) hip circumference about 8" (20.5 cm) below waist, and 20½" (52 cm) long from lower edge of waistband for all sizes.

Skirt shown measures 29½" (75 cm) at waistband.

Yarn

Worsted weight (#4 Medium).

SHOWN HERE: Classic Elite Solstice (70% organic cotton, 30% merino; 100 yd [91 m]/50 g): #2349 Calais (blue), 7 (8, 9, 9, 10) skeins.

Needles

Sizes U.S. 9, 8, 7, 6, and 5 (5.5, 5, 4.5, 4, and 3.75 mm): 32" (80 cm) circular (cir).

Adjust needle sizes if necessary to obtain the correct gauge.

Notions

Marker (m); tapestry needle; 1" (2.5 cm) wide elastic to fit around waist plus 1" (2.5 cm) overlap; sharp-point sewing needle and thread.

Gauge

20 stitches and 26 rounds = 4" (10 cm) in stockinette stitch on size 6 (4 mm) needles, worked in rounds; 19 stitches and 25 rounds = 4" (10 cm) in stockinette stitch on size 7 (4.5 mm) needles, worked in rounds; 22 sts (two patt reps) of lace pattern measure about 5·" (14 cm) wide on largest needle, worked in rounds.

Note

- *The skirt begins at the lower edge with the lace pattern worked on the largest needle. The skirt is shaped by changing to progressively smaller needles to the ribbed waist, which is worked on the smallest needle.*

STITCH GUIDE

Lace Pattern
(multiple of 11 sts)

RND 1: *P1, k1, yo, k3, sl 1, k2tog, psso, k3, yo; rep from * around.

RND 2: *P1, k10; rep from * around.

RND 3: *P1, yo, k3, k3tog, k3, yo, k1; rep from * around.

RND 4: Rep Rnd 2.

Repeat Rnds 1–4 for pattern.

Skirt

With size 9 (5.5 mm) needle, CO 165 (187, 209, 231, 253) sts. Place marker and join for working in rnds, being careful not to twist sts. Work lace patt (see Stitch Guide) until piece measures 6" (15 cm) from CO. Change to size 8 (5 mm) needle and work even as established until piece measures 11" (28 cm) from CO. Change to size 7 (4.5 mm) needle and work in St st (knit every rnd) until piece measures 17½" (44.5 cm) from CO, or 3" (7.5 cm) less than desired length to base of waistband. Change to size 6 (4 mm) needle and work even until piece measures 20½" (52 cm) from CO or desired length.

Waistband and Facing

Change to size 5 (3.75 mm) needle.

NEXT RND: K2tog, *p1, k1; rep from * —164 (186, 208, 230, 252) sts rem.

NEXT RND: *K1, p1; rep from *.

Rep the last rnd until rib section measures 1½" (3.8 cm).

TURNING RND: P4 (10, 0, 6, 12), [p2tog, p8 (9, 11, 12, 13)] 16 times—148 (170, 192, 214, 236) sts rem. Remove end-of-rnd marker and work St st (knit RS rows; purl WS rows) back and forth in rows until facing measures 1½" (3.8 cm) from turning rnd.

Loosely BO all sts.

Finishing

Block to measurements (the facing is not shown on the schematic). Fold facing to WS along turning rnd and, with yarn threaded on a tapestry needle, sew BO edge of facing to first rnd of ribbing to form casing for elastic. Thread elastic through casing, overlap ends as necessary to achieve the correct fit. Sew the overlapped ends of the elastic together with sharp-point sewing needle and thread. With yarn threaded on a tapestry needle, sew selvedges of facing tog to close opening in casing. Weave in loose ends. Block again, if desired.

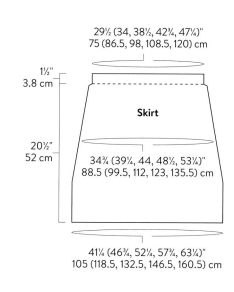

29½ (34, 38½, 42¾, 47¼)"
75 (86.5, 98, 108.5, 120) cm

1½"
3.8 cm

Skirt

20½"
52 cm

34¾ (39¼, 44, 48½, 53¼)"
88.5 (99.5, 112, 123, 135.5) cm

41¼ (46¾, 52¼, 57¾, 63¼)"
105 (118.5, 132.5, 146.5, 160.5) cm

Casting On & Binding Off Lace

by **Eunny Jang**

Adapted from "A Primer on Knitted Lace: Part Two,"
Interweave Knits, Fall 2006

Knitted lace, a fabric that consists largely of holes, will always stretch wider than its counterpart in stockinette or garter stitch. The most common methods of casting on and binding off, however, often produce an edge that's too firm and inflexible to stretch the width of a lacy fabric.

Traditional lace shawls were often designed to avoid this problem by doing away with cast-on or bound-off edges altogether. A provisional cast-on and a "live" last row allowed the piece to be finished off with a perpendicular knitted edging. But many of today's lace projects—simple lace scarves and shawls, for example—are knitted from a permanent cast-on edge to the bind-off row. The following cast-on and bind-off methods yield flexible edges with enough give to accommodate the most aggressive locking.

CASTING ON

A Note on the Long-Tail Cast-On

Conventional wisdom for increasing the elasticity of a cast-on edge has the knitter work the long-tail (Continental) method over two needles. Unfortunately, this modification doesn't provide a more elastic edge: the stitches on the needle may be larger, but the size of the knots at the base of the stitches remains the same. Only a very little yarn is used in each "knot" and between neighboring knots, yielding the same tight and inelastic edge.

To compensate, the knitter must somehow add extra yarn either to each knot formed at the base of the stitch or between knots. Leave a consistent length of yarn (¼"–½" [6–13 mm], depending on the gauge of the piece) between each stitch as you cast on, or use June Hiatt's ingenious double-needle cast-on, from her book *The Principles of Knitting: Methods and Techniques of Hand Knitting* (Touchstone, 2012), to enlarge the knots themselves.

Backward-Loop Cast-On

The backward-loop cast-on works beautifully for lace fabric because of its absolute simplicity—there are no twists or knots on the cast-on row of stitches. But it may stretch even more than the body stitches and must be pinned carefully during blocking to avoid flared or scalloped edges.

Make a loop with the working yarn and place it on the needle backward. The loops may be made with the ball end of the yarn in front or in back of the loop. The difference is almost impossible to see once worked, though you may prefer a forward loop (**Figure 1**) when the first row after cast-on is knitted and a backward loop (**Figure 2**) when it's purled.

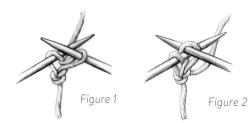

Figure 1

Figure 2

Knitted Cast-On

More solid than a backward-loop cast-on, the knitted cast-on produces an edge that is lacy and loopy and will stretch as far as you need it to. Though instructions for this cast-on often start with a slipknot loop, for a completely knotless edge, try a simple twisted loop instead.

Place a twisted loop (or slipknot) on the left needle. Knit into this stitch with the right needle (**Figure 1**), draw a new stitch through, and place it on the left needle (**Figure 2**). Repeat until the correct number of stitches has been cast on, always knitting into the last stitch you made.

Figure 1   *Figure 2*

Cable Cast-On

If there are no stitches on the needles, make a slip-knot of working yarn and place it on the needle, then use the knitted method to cast on one more stitch—two stitches on needle. Hold needle with working yarn in your left hand with the wrong side of the work facing you. *Insert right needle between the first two stitches on left needle (**Figure 1**), wrap yarn around needle as if to knit, draw yarn through (**Figure 2**), and place new loop on left needle (**Figure 3**) to form a new stitch. Repeat from * for the desired number of stitches, always working between the first two stitches on the left needle.

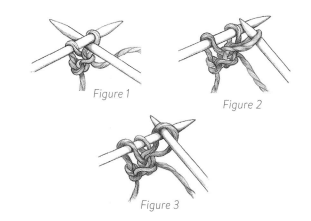

Figure 1

Figure 2

Figure 3

Emily Ocker's Circular Beginning

Make a simple loop of yarn with the short end hanging down. With a crochet hook, *draw a loop through main loop, then draw another loop through this loop. Repeat from * for each stitch to be cast on. After several inches have been worked, pull on the short end to tighten the loop and close the circle.

BINDING OFF

Many lace patterns, after pages of intricate charts and working instructions, end abruptly with a note to "bind off loosely." Although the standard k1, psso bind-off may be loosened slightly by working it with a needle many sizes larger than those used for the body, it still may not have the necessary give to stretch comfortably with the fabric. The following variations on binding off may be a little more awkward to work, but the results are worth it.

Standard Bind-Off

Knit the first stitch, *knit the next stitch (two stitches on right needle), insert left needle tip into first stitch on right needle (**Figure 1**) and lift this stitch up and over the second stitch (**Figure 2**) and off the needle (**Figure 3**). Repeat from * for the desired number of stitches.

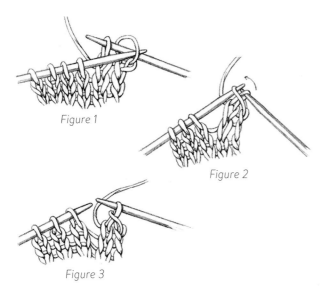

Figure 1

Figure 2

Figure 3

Modified Standard Bind-Off

If working with very large needles doesn't produce a bind-off with enough elasticity, a little extra yarn can be manually inserted as you work. Bind off as usual, making a yarnover between stitches at regular intervals (**Figure 1**) and slipping it over with the stitch being bound-off (**Figure 2**). Depending on how open and airy the body stitch is—and how far it needs to stretch—a yarnover may be inserted between every third, second, or even after every stitch.

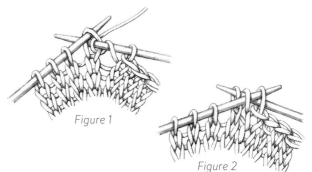

Figure 1

Figure 2

Suspended Bind-Off

Another variation on the standard method, this provides more stretch by inserting extra yarn in the bind-off. Slip one stitch, knit one stitch, *insert left needle tip into first stitch on right needle and lift the first stitch over the second, keeping the lifted stitch at the end of the left needle (**Figure 1**). Skipping the lifted stitch, knit the next stitch (**Figure 2**), then slip both stitches off the left needle—two stitches remain on right needle and one stitch has been bound off (**Figure 3**). Repeat from * until no stitches remain on left needle, then pass first stitch on right needle over second.

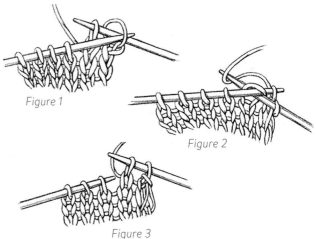

Figure 1

Figure 2

Figure 3

Elizabeth Zimmermann's Sewn Bind-Off

This sewn bind-off, which Elizabeth Zimmermann described in her book *Knitting Without Tears* (Fireside, 1973), mirrors the look of a cast-on row. Worked with carefully matched tension, it makes a tidy bound-off edge.

Break working yarn, leaving at least 1½" (3.8 cm) for every stitch to be bound off. Thread the yarn into a blunt tapestry needle small enough to pass through the live stitches without stretching them. Insert the tapestry needle into the first stitch on the needle as if to knit and slip this stitch off the knitting needle. *Insert the tapestry needle purlwise into the next two stitches, leaving them on the knitting needle (**Figure 1**), and pull the yarn through. Insert the tapestry needle into the first stitch on the needle as if to knit (**Figure 2**) and slip this stitch off the needle. Repeat from * until all stitches have been bound off.

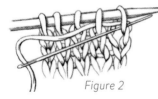

Figure 1

Figure 2

Lace Bind-Off

Sometimes called a Russian bind-off, the yielding—but very strong—edge this method creates is ideal for edges that are to be blocked into points or scallops. Though the bind-off row is worked with purl stitches, it looks right at home on the right side of a stockinette fabric—a good thing, because a bind-off worked in this way with knit stitches doesn't have the same elasticity.

Purl two stitches. *Slip the two stitches back onto the left needle, without twisting (**Figure 1**). Purl two together (**Figure 2**), purl one stitch (**Figure 3**). Repeat from * until one stitch remains; break yarn and pull through to finish.

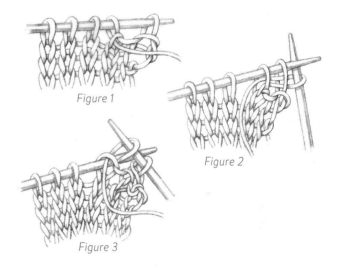

Figure 1

Figure 2

Figure 3

Arts & Crafts
cardigan

by **Amy Christoffers**

Lace meets cables in this ode to the Arts and Crafts movement. The clean lines, strong structure, and organic design elements evoke the simple forms and elegant flourishes that were a hallmark of Arts and Crafts design. Amy Christoffers uses beautiful cabled lace panels to punctuate the otherwise simple structure of this bottom-up cardigan.

Finished Size
About 32¾ (36, 39¼, 42½, 45½, 48¾)" (83 [91.5, 99.5, 108, 115.5, 124] cm) bust circumference, buttoned with 1¼" (3.2 cm) overlapped buttonband.

Cardigan shown measures 36" (91.5 cm) and is designed to be worn with slight ease.

Yarn
Worsted weight (#4 Medium).

SHOWN HERE: Peace Fleece Worsted (70% wool, 30% mohair; 200 yd [183 m]/113 g): Lauren's Coral, 5 (5, 6, 6, 7, 7) skeins.

Needles
RIBBING: Size U.S. 8 (5 mm): 24" (60 cm) circular (cir) and set of 4 or 5 double-pointed (dpn).

BODY AND SLEEVES: Size U.S. 9 (5.5 mm): 24" (60 cm) cir and set of 4 or 5 dpn.

Adjust needle sizes if necessary to obtain the correct gauge.

Notions
Markers (m); cable needle (cn); stitch holders or waste yarn; tapestry needle; five 1" (2.5 cm) buttons.

Gauge
15 sts and 22 rows = 4" (10 cm) in Rev St st with larger needles; 13 sts = 2¾" (7 cm) in Arts and Crafts Panel with larger needles.

K1, p1 Rib

Flat
(multiple of 2 sts + 1)

ROW 1: (WS) P1, *k1, p1; rep from *.

ROW 2: (RS) K1, *p1, k1; rep from *.

Rep Rows 1 and 2 for patt.

Circular
(multiple of 2 sts)

RND 1: *K1, p1; rep from *.

Rep Rnd 1 for patt.

Arts and Crafts Panel
(panel of 13 sts—also, see chart)

Flat

ROW 1: (RS) P1, k1, p1, sl 2 sts onto cn and hold in back, k1, k2 from cn, k1, sl 1 st onto cn and hold in front, k2, k1 from cn, p1, k1, p1.

ROWS 2 AND 4: (WS) K1, p1, k1, p7, k1, p1, k1.

ROW 3: K2tog, yo, p1, k1, k2tog, yo, k1, yo, ssk, k1, p1, yo, ssk.

ROW 5: P1, k1, p1, k2tog, yo, k3, yo, ssk, p1, k1, p1.

ROW 6: Rep Row 2.

Rep Rows 1–6 for patt.

Circular

RND 1: (RS) P1, k1, p1, sl 2 sts onto cn and hold in back, k1, k2 from cn, k1, sl 1 st onto cn and hold in front, k2, k1 from cn, p1, k1, p1.

RNDS 2 AND 4: P1, k1, p1, k7, p1, k1, p1.

RND 3: K2tog, yo, p1, k1, k2tog, yo, k1, yo, ssk, k1, p1, yo, ssk.

RND 5: P1, k1, p1, k2tog, yo, k3, yo, ssk, p1, k1, p1.

RND 6: Rep Rnd 2.

Rep Rnds 1–6 for patt.

Body

With smaller cir, CO 129 (141, 153, 165, 177, 189) sts. Do not join; work back and forth in rows.

Work k1, p1 rib (see Stitch Guide) until piece measures 3" (7.5 cm) from beg, ending with a WS row. Change to larger cir.

EST PATT: (RS) Work 12 (12, 12, 14, 14, 14) sts in Rev St st, work 13 sts in Arts and Crafts Panel (see Stitch Guide), work 8 (11, 14, 15, 18, 21) sts in Rev St st, pm for side, work 7 (10, 13, 14, 17, 20) sts in Rev St st, work 13 sts in Arts and Crafts Panel, work 23 (23, 23, 27, 27, 27) sts in Rev St st, 13 sts in Arts and Crafts Panel, 7 (10, 13, 14, 17, 20) sts in Rev St st, pm for side, work 8 (11, 14, 15, 18, 21) sts in Rev St st, work 13 sts in Arts and Crafts Panel, work 12 (12, 12, 14, 14, 14) sts in Rev St st.

Cont working even as est until piece measures 5" (12.5 cm) from beg, ending with a RS row.

Shape Waist

DEC ROW: (WS) Work as est to 3 sts before m, ssk, k1, sl m, k2tog, work as est to 2 sts before next m, ssk, sl m, k1, k2tog, work to end— 4 sts dec'd.

Work 11 rows even, ending with a RS row.

Rep dec row—121 (133, 145, 157, 169, 181) sts rem.

Work 17 rows even, ending with a RS row.

INC ROW: (WS) Work to 1 st before m, M1, k1, sl m, M1, work to next m, M1, sl m, k1, M1, work to end— 4 sts inc'd.

Work 11 rows even, ending with a RS row.

Rep inc row—129 (141 153, 165, 177, 189) sts.

Cont working even as est until piece measures 17" (43 cm) from beg, ending with a WS row.

DIVIDE FRONTS AND BACK: (RS) Work right front to 4 (5, 5, 6, 7, 7) sts before m, BO the next 7 (9, 9, 11, 13, 13) sts, work back to 3 (4, 4, 5, 6, 6) sts before next m, BO the next 7 (9, 9, 11, 13, 13) sts, work left front to end—29 (31, 34, 36, 38, 41) sts rem each front and 57 (61, 67, 71, 75, 81) sts rem for back. Cont working back and forth on sts for left front. Sl sts for back and right front onto st holders or waste yarn.

Left Front
Shape Neck and Armhole

DEC ROW 1: (WS) K1, ssk, work to end as est—28 (30, 33, 35, 37, 40) sts rem.

DEC ROW 2: (RS) P1, p2tog, work to last 3 sts, ssp, p1—2 sts dec'd.

NEXT ROW: Work even as est.

Rep the last 2 rows 2 (3, 4, 4, 5, 6) more times—22 (22, 23, 25, 25, 26) sts rem.

Arts and Crafts

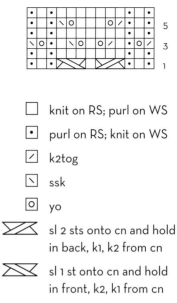

□ knit on RS; purl on WS

⊡ purl on RS; knit on WS

☑ k2tog

☒ ssk

⊡ yo

⧄ sl 2 sts onto cn and hold in back, k1, k2 from cn

⧅ sl 1 st onto cn and hold in front, k2, k1 from cn

Shape Neck

DEC ROW: (RS) Work to last 3 sts, ssp, p1—1 st dec'd.

NEXT ROW: Work even as est.

Rep the last 2 rows 7 (6, 5, 7, 6, 5) more times—14 (15, 17, 17, 18, 20) sts rem.

Cont to work even as est until armhole measures 7¾ (8, 8¼, 8½, 8¾, 9)" (19.5 [20.5, 21, 21.5, 22, 23] cm) from divide, ending with a RS row.

Shape Shoulder

Cont working as est, while shaping shoulder with short-rows as foll:

SHORT-ROW 1: (WS) Work to last 8 (9, 11, 12, 14, 16) sts, w&t (see Glossary).

SHORT-ROW 2: (RS) Work to end.

SHORT-ROW 3: Work to end of row, working wrap together with the st it wraps.

Sl all sts onto st holder or waste yarn. Break yarn and set aside.

Back

Return 57 (61, 67, 71, 75, 81) held back sts to larger cir and join yarn preparing to work a WS row.

Shape Armholes

(WS) Work 1 row.

DEC ROW: (RS) P1, p2tog, work to last 3 sts, ssp, p1—2 sts dec'd.

Rep the last 2 rows 2 (3, 4, 4, 5, 6) more times—51 (53, 57, 61, 63, 67) sts rem.

Work even until armholes measure 7¾ (8, 8¼, 8½, 8¾, 9)" (19.5 [20.5, 21, 21.5, 22, 23] cm) from divide, ending with a WS row.

Shape Shoulders

Cont working as est, while shaping shoulders with short-rows as foll:

SHORT-ROWS 1 AND 2: Work to last 8 (9, 11, 12, 14, 16) sts, w&t.

SHORT-ROWS 3 AND 4: Work to end, working wrap together with the st it wraps.

Shape Neck

NEXT ROW: (RS) Work 14 (15, 17, 17, 18, 20) sts, BO 23 (23, 23, 27, 27, 27) sts for neck back, work across rem 14 (15, 17, 17, 18, 20) sts. Sl sts onto st holder or waste yarn. Break yarn, leaving about 18" (45.5 cm) tail for three-needle BO.

Right Front

Return 29 (31, 34, 36, 38, 41) held right front sts to larger cir and join yarn preparing to work a WS row.

Shape Neck and Armhole

DEC ROW 1: (WS) Work to last 3 sts, k2tog, k1—28 (30, 33, 35, 37, 40) sts rem.

DEC ROW 2: (RS) P1, p2tog, work to last 3 sts, ssp, p1—2 sts dec'd.

NEXT ROW: Work even as est.

Rep the last 2 rows 2 (3, 4, 4, 5, 6) more times—22 (22, 23, 25, 25, 26) sts rem.

Shape Neck

DEC ROW: (RS) P1, p2tog, work to end—1 st dec'd.

NEXT ROW: Work even as est.

Rep the last 2 rows 7 (6, 5, 7, 6, 5) more times—14 (15, 17, 17, 18, 20) sts rem.

Cont to work even as est until armhole measures 7¾ (8, 8¼, 8½, 8¾, 9)" (19.5 [20.5, 21, 21.5, 22, 23] cm) from divide, ending with a WS row.

Shape Shoulder

Cont working as est, while shaping shoulder with short-rows as foll:

SHORT-ROW 1: (RS) Work to last 8 (9, 11, 12, 14, 16) sts, w&t.

SHORT-ROW 2: (WS) Work to end.

SHORT-ROW 3: Work to end of row, working wrap together with the st it wraps.

Sl sts onto st holder or waste yarn. Break yarn, leaving about 18" (45.5 cm) tail for three-needle BO.

Sleeve (make 2)

With smaller dpn, CO 36 (36, 40, 44, 48, 52) sts. Divide sts evenly over 3 or 4 dpn, pm for beg of rnd and join to work in the rnd, being careful not to twist sts.

Work k1, p1 rib until piece measures 3" (7.5 cm) from beg. Change to larger dpn.

EST PATT: Work 12 (12, 14, 16, 18, 20) sts in Rev St st, work 13 sts in Arts and Crafts Panel, work 11 (11, 13, 15, 17, 19) sts in Rev St st.

Cont working as est for 11 (11, 11, 5, 5, 5) more rnds.

Shape Sleeve

INC RND: P1, M1P, work as est to end, M1P—2 sts inc'd.

Work 13 (11, 9, 7, 7, 7) rnds even as est.

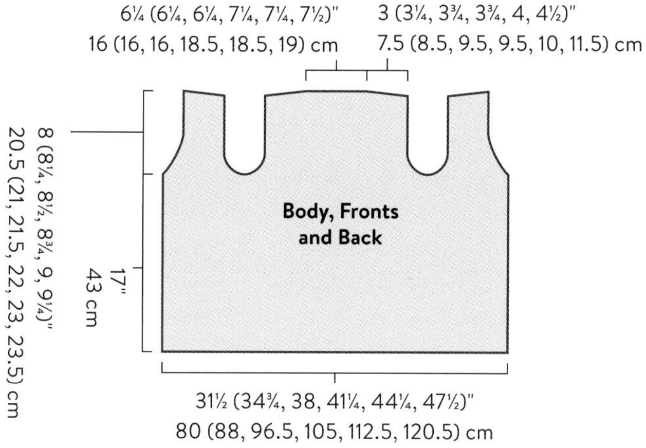
6¼ (6¼, 6¼, 7¼, 7¼, 7½)"
16 (16, 16, 18.5, 18.5, 19) cm
3 (3¼, 3¾, 3¾, 4, 4½)"
7.5 (8.5, 9.5, 9.5, 10, 11.5) cm
8 (8¼, 8½, 8¾, 9, 9¼)"
20.5 (21, 21.5, 22, 23, 23.5) cm
17"
43 cm
Body, Fronts and Back
31½ (34¾, 38, 41¼, 44¼, 47½)"
80 (88, 96.5, 105, 112.5, 120.5) cm

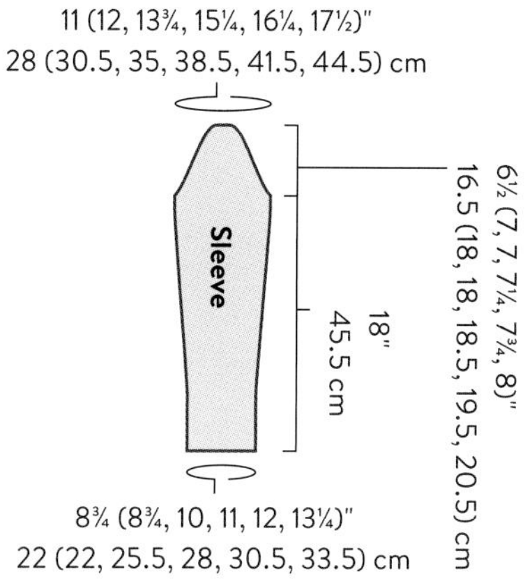
11 (12, 13¾, 15¼, 16¼, 17½)"
28 (30.5, 35, 38.5, 41.5, 44.5) cm
6½ (7, 7, 7¼, 7¾, 8)"
16.5 (18, 18, 18.5, 19.5, 20.5) cm
Sleeve
18"
45.5 cm
8¾ (8¾, 10, 11, 12, 13¼)"
22 (22, 25.5, 28, 30.5, 33.5) cm

Rep the last 14 (12, 10, 8, 8, 8) rnds 3 (5, 6, 7, 7, 7) more times—44 (48, 54, 60, 64, 68) sts.

Work even as est until sleeve measures 18" (45.5 cm) from beg, ending last rnd 3 (4, 4, 5, 6, 6) sts before m.

Shape Cap

BO the next 7 (9, 9, 11, 13, 13) sts—37 (39, 45, 49, 51, 55) sts rem.

Cont working back and forth in rows.

NEXT ROW: (WS) Work even as est.

DEC ROW: (RS) P1, p2tog, work as est to last 3 sts, ssp, p1—2 sts dec'd.

Rep the last 2 rows 2 (3, 4, 4, 5, 6) more times—31 (31, 35, 39, 39, 41) sts rem.

[Work 3 rows even, then rep dec row] 5 (5, 3, 2, 2, 1) times—21 (21, 29, 35, 35, 39) sts rem.

[Work 1 row even, then rep dec row] 3 (3, 5, 8, 8, 10) times—15 (15, 19, 19, 19, 19) sts rem.

DEC ROW: (WS) K1, ssk, work as est to last 3 sts, k2tog, k1—2 sts dec'd.

DEC ROW: (RS) P1, p2tog, work as est to last 3 sts, ssp, p1—2 sts dec'd.

Rep the last 2 rows 0 (0, 1, 1, 1, 1) more times, then work 1 more WS dec row—9 sts rem.

BO rem sts.

Finishing

Block pieces to measurements.

JOIN SHOULDERS: Return 14 (15, 17, 17, 18, 20) held sts from right front and right back onto larger dpn and with RS held together join sts using the three-needle BO (see Glossary). Rep for left shoulder.

With yarn threaded on a tapestry needle, sew sleeves into armholes.

NECKBAND: With smaller cir, and RS facing, beg at lower edge of right front, pick up and knit 68 sts to beg of neck shaping, 28 (30, 32, 34, 36, 38) sts evenly along right front neck to shoulder seam, pm, pick up and knit 23 (23, 23, 27, 27, 27) sts across back neck, pm, pick up and knit 28 (30, 32, 34, 36, 38) sts evenly along left front neck, then 68 sts to lower edge—215 (219, 223, 231, 235, 239) sts.

Shape Collar

Work in k1, p1 rib and shape using short-rows as foll:

SHORT-ROW 1: (WS) Work k1, p1 rib to second m, sl m, work 6 more sts in k1, p1 rib, w&t.

SHORT-ROW 2: (RS) Work 35 (35, 35, 39, 39, 39) sts, w&t.

SHORT-ROWS 3 AND 4: Work in k1, p1 rib to wrapped st, work the next st with the wrap, then work 3 (3, 3, 5, 5, 5) more sts, w&t.

SHORT-ROWS 5 AND 6: Work in k1, p1 rib to wrapped st, work the next st with the wrap, then work 1 (3, 3, 3, 5, 5) sts w&t.

SHORT-ROWS 7 AND 8: Work in k1, p1 rib to wrapped st, work the next st with the wrap, then work 1 (1, 3, 3, 3, 5) sts, w&t.

SHORT-ROWS 9 AND 10: Work in k1, p1 rib to wrapped st, work the next st with the wrap, then work 1 st, w&t.

Rep the last 2 short-rows 4 more times—71 (75, 79, 87, 91, 95) sts used for collar; 72 sts each side of wrapped sts.

NEXT ROW: (WS) Work k1, p1 rib to end.

Work 2 rows even in k1, p1 rib, ending with a WS row.

BUTTONHOLE ROW: (RS) [K1, p1] 2 times, ssk, [yo] twice, *[k1, p1] 7 times, ssk, [yo] twice; rep from * 3 more times, k1, [p1, k1] to end.

NEXT ROW: (WS) *Work in patt to double yo, purl into double yo dropping the extra wrap; rep from * 4 more times, work to end in patt.

Cont in patt for 2 more rows, ending with a WS row. BO all sts in patt.

Weave in loose ends. Sew buttons opposite buttonholes.

Get Inspired

Built in London in the mid-1800s, the Red House is a classic example from the Arts and Crafts movement. Rejecting the idea that good craftsmanship came only from ornate machine-made items, the movement centered on the notion that simpler hand-made designs, created by an individual or small group, were far superior. This style often featured British flora and fauna motifs and certain ideals from the Gothic Revival period such as simple, bold frames, medieval-like color schemes, minimal ornamentation, and steep roofs.

Rosebud
faroese-style shawl

by **Margaret Stove**

One of the more traditional projects in the book, this shawl is truly breathtaking. Based on the traditional Faroese method, it fits neatly over the shoulders without slipping. A cascade of diamonds flows down the center back to the tip of the lower point. Knit in ultra-luxurious qiviut lace yarn, the shawl is intensely warm yet light as a puff of air.

Finished Size
About 19" (48.5 cm) long from center of upper edge to tip of center back point and 38" (96.5 cm) wide across top edge, after blocking.

Yarn
Laceweight (#0 Lace).

SHOWN HERE: Moco Qiviut Merino Silk Lace (70% qiviut, 20% merino, 10% silk; 300 yd [274 m]/1 oz [28 g]): cranberry, 2 skeins.

Needles
U.S. size 6 (4 mm): 32" (80 cm) circular (cir).

Adjust needle size if necessary to obtain the correct gauge.

Notions
Markers (m); set of 2 double-pointed needles (dpn) same size as main needle to hold sts for grafting (optional); tapestry needle.

Gauge
20 sts and 34 rows = 4" (10 cm) in garter st, washed and blocked.

Notes
- *The shawl begins at the pointed lower edge and is worked upward with a side panel section on each side of the center gusset and garter-stitch borders at each selvedge.*

- *The lower edging points are worked by casting on enough stitches for the entire zigzag edge, then each individual point is worked separately, back and forth in short-rows, to gradually fill in the V of the point before proceeding to the next point.*

Notes continued

- *After the side panels have been decreased to a few remaining stitches, the top garter-stitch border is worked back and forth in short-rows, joining to the live stitches across the top of the shawl as it is worked.*

- *The points and lower border of this shawl can be adapted to make a full-size square worked from the outer edge to the center in 4 triangular sections. For each section, work 5 points and the lower border, then continue in garter stitch to the center, decreasing 1 stitch at each side of all 4 garter-stitch sections every other row.*

STITCH GUIDE

Sl 2, K1, P2sso

Sl 2 sts as if to k2tog, k1, pass 2 slipped sts over—2 sts dec'd.

K2tog F&B

Knit 2 sts tog but do not remove from left-hand needle, then knit the same 2 sts tog through their back loops—2 sts made from 2 sts.

Sl 2, Kpk, P2sso

Sl 2 sts as if to k2tog, work [k1, p1, k1] all in next st, pass 2 slipped sts over 3 sts just worked—3 sts made from 3 sts.

Sl 1, K3, Pass Sl St Over 3 Sts

Sl 1 st kwise, knit the next 3 sts, pass the slipped st over the 3 sts just knit—1 st dec'd.

K2tog with Inc

On WS, k2tog but do not remove sts from left-hand needle, knit into first st, then knit into second st, then slip both sts from needle tog—2 sts inc'd to 3 sts.

Side Panel Decrease Row

Work each side panel as foll: (RS) Yo, [sl 2, k1, p2sso], yo, ssk, knit to 5 sts before next m, k2tog, yo, [sl 2, k1, p2sso], yo—2 sts dec'd in each side panel.

Pointed Edging

CO 329 sts very loosely. Knit 4 rows. **note:** *The 11 points are worked over groups of 28 sts each, with an 8-st garter border at each side and a single 5-st lace motif inside the first border to balance the pattern. Do not wrap any sts for the short-rows; the holes created by turning at the end of each short-row become part of the lace patt.*

Beg first point as foll:

NEXT ROW: (RS) K8 for side border, work next 5 sts to balance patt as k2tog, yo, k1, yo, ssk, work Row 1 of Point chart (page 108) over next 15 sts, turn.

NEXT ROW: (WS) Work Row 2 of chart over 7 sts (dec to 5 sts as shown), turn.

NEXT ROW: Work Row 3 of chart over next 6 sts, turn.

Cont in this manner until Row 19 of chart has been completed, but do not turn at end of last row—

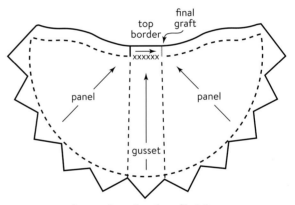

Arrows show direction of knitting.
Xs indicate sts joined to top border.

8 border sts and 5 balancing sts at beg of row; 26 sts in first point; 288 sts rem unworked at end of row. Work Rows 1–19 of Point chart over next group of 28 sts for second point (dec to 26 sts in Row 1). Work 3rd through 11th points in the same manner. After completing Row 19 of the 11th point, knit the last 8 sts for side border—307 sts rem; 26 sts each in 11 points; 5 balancing sts; 8 border sts each side.

NEXT ROW: (WS) K9 (side border), place marker (pm), k5, [p5, k4, p1, k4, p5, k7] 10 times, p5, k4, p1, k4, p5, k5, pm, k9 (side border).

Side Panels and Center Gusset

Establish patts from Row 1 of Lower Border (page 109) and Center charts (page108) as foll: (RS) K9, sl m, *work 27 sts before patt rep of Lower Border chart once (dec to 26 sts as shown), work 26-st patt 3 times, work 28 sts after patt rep once (dec to 27 sts as shown),* pm, work Center chart over 23 sts, pm; rep from * to * once more for second side panel, pm, k9 (side border).

Keeping 9 border sts at each side in garter st, work Rows 2–26 of charts—235 sts rem; 95 sts each side panel section; 27 sts center gusset; 9 border sts each side.

NEXT ROW: (RS) K6, ssk, k1, slip marker (sl m), work Row 27 of established patts to last 9 sts, sl m, k1, k2tog, k6—8 border sts each side.

Work Rows 28–42 of charts—194 sts rem; 79 sts each side panel; 20 sts center gusset; 8 border sts each side.

NEXT ROW: (RS) K8, sl m, work side panel dec row (see Stitch Guide), sl m, work Row 43 of Center chart, sl m; work side panel dec row, sl m, k8—77 sts each side panel.

note: *Work foll WS side panel rows in garter st. Work 3 rows in patt, dec 2 sts each side panel on next RS row, and end with Row 46 of Center chart—187 sts rem; 75 sts each side panel; 21 sts center gusset; 8 border sts each side.*

NEXT ROW: (RS) K5, ssk, k1, sl m, work side panel dec row, sl m, work Row 47 of Center chart, sl m, work side panel dec row, sl m, k1, k2tog, k5—73 sts each side panel; 7 border sts each side.

Cont in patt, dec 2 sts in each side panel every RS row until Row 62 of Center chart has been completed—151 sts rem; 59 sts each side panel; 19 sts center gusset; 7 border sts each side.

NEXT ROW: (RS) K4, ssk, k1, sl m, *yo, [sl 2, k1, p2sso], yo, ssk, [k5, k2tog] 7 times, k2tog, yo, [sl 2, k1, p2sso], yo,* sl m, work Row 63 of

Center chart, sl m; rep from * to * for second side panel, sl m, k1, k2tog, k4—131 sts rem; 50 sts each side panel; 19 sts center gusset; 6 border sts each side.

Cont in patt, dec 2 sts in each side panel every RS row until Row 72 of Center chart has been completed—115 sts rem; 42 sts each side panel; 19 sts center gusset; 6 border sts each side.

NEXT ROW: (RS) K6, sl m, *yo, [sl 2, k1, p2sso], yo, ssk, [k3, k2tog] 6 times, k2, k2tog, yo, [sl 2, k1, p2sso], yo,* sl m, work Row 73 of Center chart, sl m; rep from * to * for second side panel, sl m, k6—101 sts rem; 34 sts each side panel; 21 sts center gusset; 6 border sts each side.

Cont in patt, dec 2 sts in each side panel every RS row, until Row 84 of Center chart has been completed—75 sts rem; 24 sts each side panel; 15 sts center gusset; 6 border sts each side.

NEXT ROW: (RS) K3, ssk, k1, sl m, *yo, [sl 2, k1, p2sso], yo, ssk, [k3, k2tog] 2 times, k4, k2tog, yo, [sl 2, k1, p2sso], yo,* sl m, work Row 85 of Center chart, sl m; rep from * to * for second side panel, sl m, k1, k2tog, k3—65 sts rem; 20 sts each

side panel; 15 sts center gusset; 5 border sts each side.

Cont in patt, dec 2 sts in each side panel every RS row, until Row 98 of Center chart has been completed—39 sts rem; 8 sts each side panel; 13 sts center gusset; 5 border sts each side.

NEXT ROW: (RS) K5, sl m, *yo, [sl 2, k1, p2sso], yo, ssk, yo, [sl 2, k1, p2sso], yo,* sl m, work Row 99 of Center chart, sl m; rep from * to * for second side panel, sl m, k5—7 sts each side panel.

NEXT ROW: (WS) Work even in patt.

NEXT ROW: (RS) K5, sl m, *yo, ssk, [sl 2, k1, p2sso], k2tog, yo,* sl m, work Row 101 of Center chart, sl m; rep from * to * for second side panel, sl m, k5—29 sts rem; 5 sts each side panel; 9 sts center gusset; 5 border sts each side.

NEXT ROW: (WS) Work even in patt.

NEXT ROW: (RS) Removing markers as you come to them, k4, k2tog, yo, [sl 2, k1, p2sso], yo, k2tog (last side panel st tog with 1 center gusset st), k7, k2tog (last center gusset st tog with 1 side panel st), yo, [sl 2, k1, p2sso], yo, k2tog, k4—25 sts rem.

Point

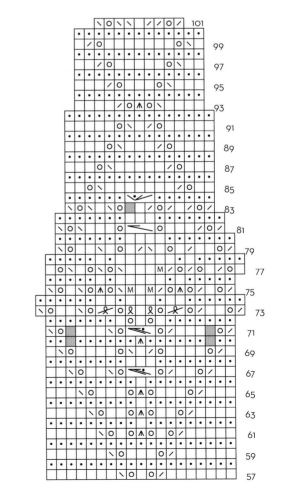

Center

Top Border

The top border is worked back and forth in short-rows, without wrapping any sts at the turning points, and joining 1 border st to 1 live st from the top edge at the end of each WS short-row.

SHORT-ROW 1: (WS) K8, k2tog, turn—1 st joined.

SHORT-ROW 2: (RS) K1, yo, [sl 2, k1, p2sso], yo, k5.

Rep Short-rows 1 and 2 six more times—18 sts rem. Knit 1 WS row across all sts. Break yarn, leaving a long tail for grafting. Place 9 sts each on 2 dpn or 9 sts on each end of the circular needle. Hold needles tog with WS of fabric touching and RS of shawl facing out. Use tail threaded on a tapestry needle to graft sts tog using Kitchener st (see Glossary).

Finishing

Wash and block to measurements. Weave in ends.

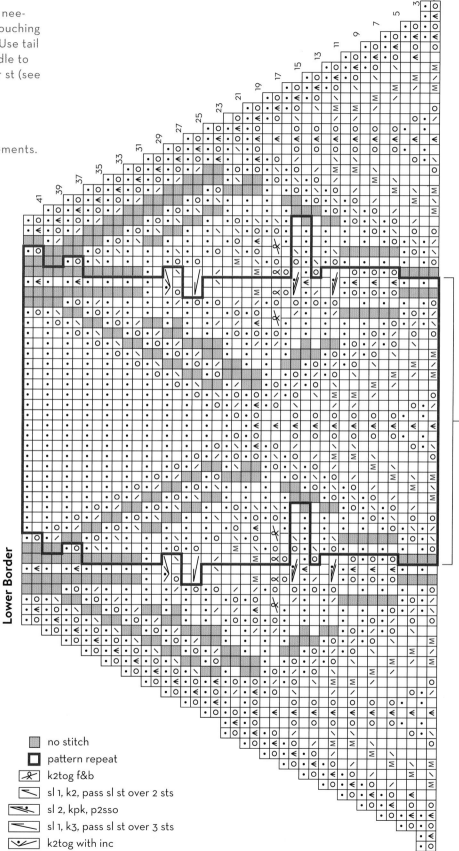

Lower Border

work 3 times

☐ k on RS rows and all rnds; p on WS rows

⊡ p on RS rows and all rnds; k on WS rows

🛇 k1tbl

☉ yo

╱ k2tog on RS rows and all rnds; p2tog on WS rows

╲ ssk on RS rows and all rnds; ssp on WS rows

🛆 sl 2, k1, p2sso

Ⓜ M1 (see Glossary)

▨ st left unworked during short-rows

▨ no stitch

☐ pattern repeat

✂ k2tog f&b

╲ sl 1, k2, pass sl st over 2 sts

⋉ sl 2, kpk, p2sso

╲ sl 1, k3, pass sl st over 3 sts

⌣ k2tog with inc

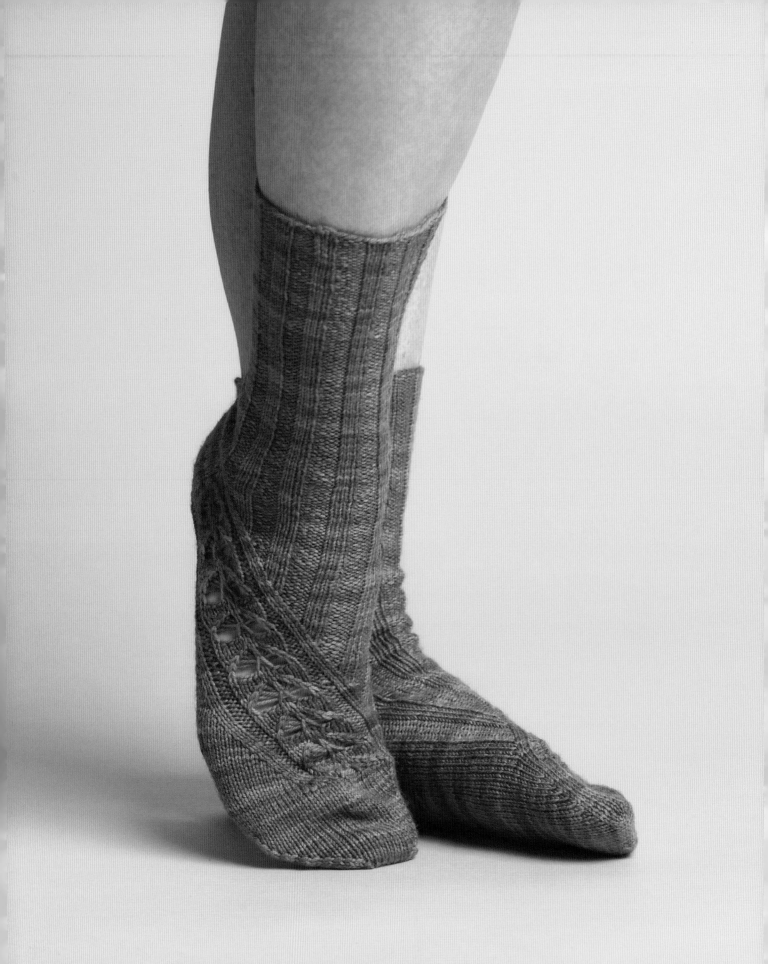

Kai-Mei
socks

by **Cookie A.**

According to the inimitable Cookie A., Kai-Mei is a physicist, a mother, a feminist, and a runner to boot. And somehow she manages to pull it all together—just like these socks. A straightforward ribbed cuff leads to a lace pattern at the gusset stitch pick-up. Shifting the gusset decreases to one side of the lace panel causes it to angle across the top of the foot, demonstrating that the path taken need not be traditional.

Finished Size

LEG CIRCUMFERENCE: 8" (20.5 cm), slightly stretched.

FOOT CIRCUMFERENCE: 8" (20.5 cm), slightly stretched.

This pattern can be resized by adding or removing ribs in the cuff. The foot is worked the same, except the top and bottom of the foot will be narrower/wider, and the shaping will have to be shifted accordingly.

Yarn

Fingering weight (#1 Super Fine).

SHOWN HERE: Dream in Color Smooshy (100% superwash merino wool; 450 yd [411 m]/4 oz): Happy Forest, 1 skein.

Needles

U.S. size 1 (2.25 mm): circular (cir) or double-pointed (dpn).

Adjust needle size if necessary to obtain the correct gauge.

Notions

Markers (m; optional); tapestry needle.

Gauge

33 stitches and 53 rounds = 4" (10 cm) in stockinette stitch in the round.

33 stitches and 53 rounds = 4" (10 cm) in 3x3 ribbing in the round, slightly stretched.

Note

- *Left and right socks are mirror images of each other. Directions are the same for both socks except where specified.*

Leg

CO 66 sts. Being careful not to twist stitches, join for working in the round and place marker (pm) for beg of rnd.

Work k3, p3 ribbing until piece measures 6½" (16.5 cm).

Heel

Heel Flap

Divide for heel flap as foll: Place last 33 sts worked on hold for top of foot; rem 33 sts will be worked back and forth for heel flap.

ROW 1: (RS) [K3, p3] 5 times, k3.

ROW 2: Sl 1 purlwise (pwise) with yarn in front (wyf), p32.

ROW 3: [Sl 1 pwise with yarn in back (wyb), k1] 16 times, k1.

Rep Rows 2 and 3 until heel flap measures 2¼–2½" (5.5–6.5 cm), ending after Row 2.

Turn Heel

Work back and forth in short-rows to shape heel.

SHORT-ROW 1: (RS): Sl 1 pwise wyb, k17, ssk, k1, turn.

SHORT-ROW 2: Sl 1 pwise wyf, p4, p2tog, p1, turn.

SHORT-ROW 3: Sl 1 pwise wyb, knit to 1 st before gap created on previous row, ssk (1 st from each side of gap), k1, turn.

SHORT-ROW 4: Sl 1 pwise wyf, purl to 1 st before gap created on previous row, p2tog (1 st from each side of gap), p1, turn.

Rep Short-rows 3 and 4 until all sts have been worked—19 heel sts rem.

Shape Gussets

note: *Where possible, arrange sts so that marker placement occurs between needles.*

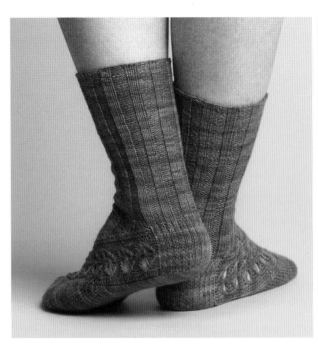

Right Sock Only

SET-UP RND: Sl 1 pwise wyb, k9, pm for beg of rnd, k9, pick up and knit 1 st in each sl st along edge of heel flap, pick up and knit 1 st between heel flap and top of foot, pm for panel; resume working in the rnd over held sts by working [p3, k3] 5 times, p3, pm for left side of foot; pick up and knit 1 st between top of foot and heel flap and 1 st in each sl st along edge of heel flap, k10 to end of round.

RND 1: Knit to 16 sts before panel m, pm for right side of foot, work Row 1 of Panel chart, k1, ssk, work rib patt to left m, ssk, knit to end—2 sts dec'd.

RND 2: Knit to right m, work next row of Panel chart, k1, sl m, k1, work in rib patt to left m, knit to end.

RND 3: Knit to right m, work next row of Panel chart, k1, ssk, work in rib patt to left m, ssk, knit to end—2 sts dec'd.

Rep Rnds 2 and 3 until 66 sts rem.

Left Sock Only

SET-UP RND: Sl 1 pwise wyb, k9, pm for beg of rnd, k9, pick up and knit 1 st in each sl st along edge of heel flap, pick up and knit 1 st between heel flap and instep, pm for right side of foot; resume working in the rnd on held sts by working [p3, k3] 5 times, p3, pick up and knit 1 st between top of foot and heel flap, pm for panel; pick up and knit 1 st in each sl st along edge of heel flap, k10 to end of round.

RND 1: Knit to 2 sts before right m, k2tog, work in rib patt to 2 sts before panel m, k2tog, k1, work Row 1 of Panel chart, pm for left side of foot, knit to end—2 sts dec'd.

RND 2: Knit to right m, sl m, work in rib patt to 1 st before panel m, k1, sl m, k1, work next row of Panel chart, sl m, knit to end.

RND 3: Knit to 2 sts before right m, k2tog, sl m, work in rib patt to 2 sts before panel m, k2tog, sl m, k1, work next row of Panel chart, sl m, knit to end—2 sts dec'd.

Panel
(panel of 15 sts; 8 rnd rep)

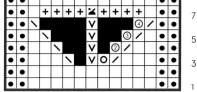

Rep Rnds 2 and 3 until 66 sts remain.

Foot
Right Sock Only

RND 1: Knit to right m, work next rnd of Panel chart, k1, sl m, work rib patt to left m, knit to end.

RND 2: Knit to 2 sts before right m, make 1 (M1; see Glossary), k2, work next rnd of Panel chart, k1, ssk, work in rib patt to m, sl m, knit to end.

Rep Rnds 1 and 2 until foot measures 2" (5 cm) less than desired length from back of heel, ending after Rnd 1, 2, or 8 of Panel chart or when panel and left markers are separated by only 1 st.

If panel marker and left markers are separated by 1 st, remove left m. Rep Rnd 3 only until foot measures 2" (5 cm) less than desired length from back of heel, ending after Rnd 1, 2, or 8 of Panel chart.

RND 3: Knit to right m, sl m, work next rnd of Panel chart, k2, sl m, k to end of round.

Left Sock Only

RND 1: Knit to right m, work in rib patt to panel m, k1, work next rnd of Panel chart, sl m, knit to end.

RND 2: Knit to right m, work in rib patt to 2 sts before panel m, k2tog,

k1, work next rnd of Panel chart, sl m, k2, M1, knit to end.

Rep Rnds 1 and 2 until foot measures 2" (5 cm) less than desired length from back of heel, ending after Rnd 1, 2, or 8 of Panel chart or when right and panel markers are separated by only 1 st.

If right marker and panel markers are separated by 1 st, remove panel m. Work Rnd 3 until foot measures 2" (5 cm) less than desired length from back of heel, ending after Rnd 1, 2, or 8 of Panel chart.

RND 3: Knit to right m, k2, work next rnd of Panel chart, knit to end.

Toe
Right Sock Only

Remove all m except for left m, count 33 sts from left m, and pm for new right side/beginning of round. Knit to right m.

Left Sock Only

Remove all m except for right m, count 33 sts from right m, and pm for new left side. Knit to right m (new beg of rnd).

Both Socks

RND 1: Knit.

RND 2: K1, ssk, knit to 3 sts before left m, k2tog, k1, k1, ssk, knit to 3 sts before right m, k2tog, k1—4 sts dec'd.

Rep Rnds 1 and 2 eleven more times—18 sts rem. Divide sts evenly over 2 needles so that there are 9 sts each for top of foot and sole.

Finish

Cut yarn, leaving a 12" (30 cm) tail. With tail threaded on a tapestry needle, use the Kitchener st (see Glossary) to graft sts. Weave in ends.

Chart key:

☐ knit

⊡ purl

☒ pick up 4 strands of dropped yarnovers. Purl 4 strands together with next stitch

◯ yarnover. Drop yarnover on next row

② yarnover 2 times. Drop yarnovers on next row

③ yarnover 3 times. Drop yarnovers on next row

④ yarnover 4 times. Drop yarnovers on next row

╲ ssk

╱ k2tog

Ⅴ sl st pwise wyb

■ no stitch

✛ CO 1 stitch using backward-loop cast-on

☐ pattern repeat

Bethe
shawlette

by **Angela Tong**

Traditional Shetland methods merge with contemporary styling in a one-skein shawlette. The garter-stitch body is worked first, then stitches for the trellis border are picked up along the bottom edge. Finally, a knitted-on edging with petit bobbles creates textural interest. Don't be put off by the number of bobbles—once you have a rhythm going, you can cruise through pretty quickly.

Finished Size

About 50" (127 cm) wide and 12" (30.5 cm) deep, after blocking.

Yarn

Fingering weight (#1 Super Fine).

SHOWN HERE: Lorna's Laces Shepherd Sock (80% wool, 20% nylon; 435 yd [398 m]/100 g): Manzanita, 1 skein.

Needles

Size U.S. 6 (4 mm): 47" (120 cm) circular (cir).

Adjust needle size if necessary to obtain the correct gauge.

Notions

Tapestry needle; blocking pins; blocking wires (optional).

Gauge

19 stitches and 54 rows = 4" (10 cm) in garter stitch, blocked.

Notes

- *This shawl is made using the traditional Shetland construction method.*

- *The bobble edging is knitted on. You may find it easier to work with a double-pointed needle as the working needle for the edging.*

Make Bobble (MB)

Work (k1, p1) 3 times into same st, sl first 5 sts on right-hand needle over 6th st.

Shawl

Garter-Stitch Body

Make a slipknot on needle—1 st.

ROW 1: Yo, k1—2 sts.

ROW 2: Yo, k2—3 sts.

ROW 3: Yo, k1, k1f&b, knit to end—2 sts inc'd.

Rep Row 3 every row 100 times—205 sts.

BO all sts loosely except for last st; do not break yarn. With 1 st on right needle, pick up, from back to front, the 104 yo loops along the curved edge of the shawl (do not knit any of these sts yet). Go back to the corner where the yarn is attached and knit across—105 sts.

NEXT ROW: (WS) Knit.

NEXT ROW: (RS) *K1, yo; rep from * to last st, k1—209 sts.

Trellis Lace Section

ROW 1: (WS) Purl.

ROW 2: (RS) K1, *yo, k2tog; rep from * to end.

ROW 3: (WS) Purl.

ROW 4: (RS) *Ssk, yo; rep from * to last st, k1.

ROWS 5–12: Rep Rows 1–4 two more times.

Garter Ridge

ROWS 13 AND 15: (WS) Purl.

ROWS 14 AND 16: (RS) Purl.

Rep Rows 1–12 of trellis lace section once more. Knit 2 rows.

Bobble Edging

note: *The edging will be joined to the body of the shawl at the end of Rows 2 and 4. The last k2tog includes 1 edging st and 1 body st.*

With the yarn that is still attached to the body of the shawl, use the backward-loop method (see Glossary) to CO 6 sts. Turn work and knit back across 5 of the new sts, then k2tog (last st of edging will be joined to first st of the body of the shawl). Turn work and proceed with edging as foll:

ROW 1: K3, yo, k2tog, k1.

ROW 2: Sl 1 pwise, k2, yo, [k2tog] twice.

ROW 3: K3, yo, k2tog, k1.

ROW 4: MB (see Stitch Guide), k2, yo, [k2tog] twice.

Rep Rows 1–4 until only 6 edging sts rem. BO all sts.

Finishing

Weave in all ends. Wet-block piece to finished measurements using pins and blocking wires.

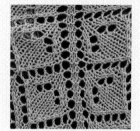

Framework
shawl

- -

by **Mercedes Tarasovich-Clark**

As she thought about classic triangular shawls, Mercedes Tarasovich-Clark wondered what could be added or taken away from the shape to create something new. Here, the triangle is both reduced by casting on for flat-topped panels of lace and expanded by bringing in a third panel to make a longer wrap.

Finished Size
About 47" (119.5 cm) wide at widest point of each segment and 15" (38 cm) deep from CO edge to BO points.

Yarn
Fingering weight (#1 Super Fine).

SHOWN HERE: Quince and Co. Tern (75% wool, 25% silk; 221 yd [202 m]/50 g): #146 Kelp, 3 skeins.

Needles
Size U.S. 8 (5 mm): 32" (80 cm) circular.

Adjust needle size if necessary to obtain the correct gauge.

Notions
Markers (m); tapestry needle.

Gauge
14 stitches and 18 rows = 4" (10 cm) in lace pattern stitch.

Notes

- On each repeat of Row 25 of the Lace chart, the shawl will expand by 4 stitches in each segment, instead of the standard 2 stitches, to keep motifs aligned. On Row 47 of the chart, work [Stitches 1–17 as charted, repeat Stitches 4–17 eight more times, then work Stitches 40–55] in each section (ignore the gray-shaded portion, Stitches 18–39); 20 stitches are increased in each section across Row 47.

STITCH GUIDE

All RS rows

[K2, sl m, work charted patt to m, sl m] 3 times, k2.

All WS rows

[K2, sl m, work charted patt to m, sl m] 3 times, k2.

Shawl

CO 152 sts.

SET-UP ROW: [K2, place marker (pm), k48, pm] 3 times, k2.

Knit 3 rows.

Work Rows 1–12 of the Lace chart once, then Rows 7–12 four times—257 sts. Work Rows 13–24 of the Lace chart once, then Rows 25–34 twice—365 sts. Work Rows 35–48 of the Lace chart once—443 sts. Using the Decrease method (see Glossary), BO all sts.

Finishing

Weave in all ends. Block piece to finished measurements.

Lace

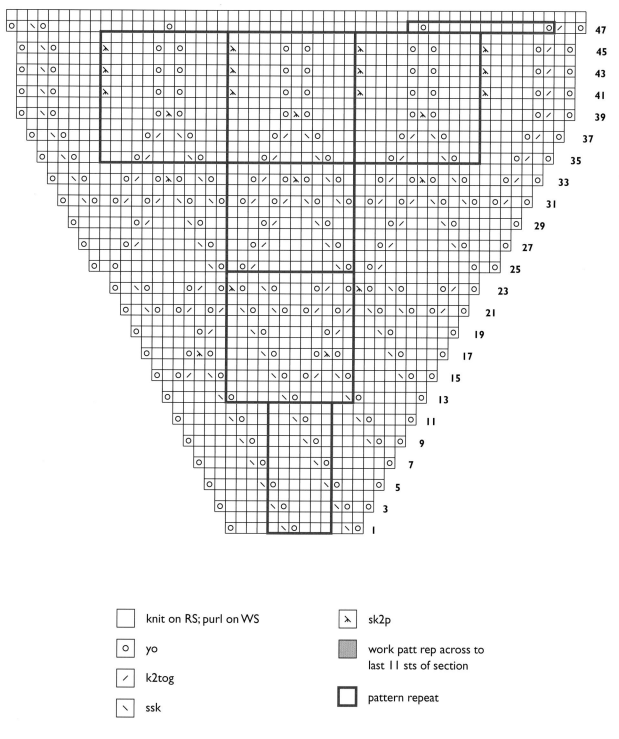

	knit on RS; purl on WS			sk2p
	yo			work patt rep across to last 11 sts of section
	k2tog			pattern repeat
	ssk			

Greenery
beret

- -

by **Melissa LaBarre**

This beret uses a pretty variation of a classic Shetland feather-and-fan stitch. The soft ripples, created by increases and decreases in the pattern, complement hand-dyed and semisolid yarns and create an interesting, undulating shape. A ribbed band keeps the hat securely on the head.

Finished Size

17½" (44.5 cm) circumference at brim, unstretched; to fit 18–22" (45.5–56 cm) head circumference.

Yarn

DK weight (#3 Light).

SHOWN HERE: Manos del Uruguay Silk Blend (70% merino, 30% silk; 150 yd [135 m]/50 g): #3204 lawn, 2 skeins.

Needles

RIBBING: U.S. size 4 (3.5 mm): 16" (40 cm) circular (cir) needle.

BODY: U.S. size 7 (4.5 mm): 16" cir and set of 4 double-pointed (dpn).

Adjust needle sizes if necessary to obtain the correct gauge.

Notions

Stitch marker (m); tapestry needle.

Gauge

23 sts and 36 rnds = 4" (10 cm) in k1, p1 ribbing, unstretched with smaller needles; 20 sts and 28 rnds = 4" (10 cm) in lace patt with larger needles.

Ribbing

With smaller cir needle, CO 100 sts. Place marker (pm) for beg of rnd and join for working in the rnd, being careful not to twist sts.

RND 1: *K1, p1; rep from * to end.

Rep last rnd 12 more times.

NEXT RND: (inc rnd): *K1, k1f&b; rep from * to end—150 sts.

Change to larger cir needle.

Body

Work Lace Fan chart 2 times.

Shape Crown

note: *Change to dpns when there are too few sts to work comfortably on cir needle.*

Work Decrease chart—20 sts rem.

NEXT RND: (decrease rnd) *K2tog; rep from * to end—10 sts rem.

Rep the last rnd once more—5 sts rem.

Break yarn, leaving an 8" (20.5 cm) tail. With tail threaded on tapestry needle, draw through rem sts, pull snug to tighten, and fasten off inside.

Finishing

Weave in ends. Dampen hat with water or steam and block stretched over a dinner plate to shape beret.

Decrease

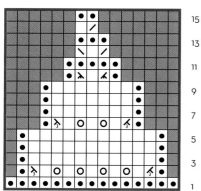

Lace Fan

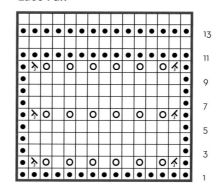

	knit
•	purl
O	yo
⚶	k4tog
⚵	sl 1, k3tog, psso
⚴	k3tog
⚳	sl 1, k2tog, psso
╱	k2tog
╲	ssk
▢	pattern repeat

Using a Smaller Needle for Rib and Brims

Frequently in hat patterns, you will notice that the ribbed trims or brims are worked on a smaller needle than the body of the hat. Ribbed edges can get stretched out with wear, and using a smaller needle makes a denser fabric and helps to prevent this from happening. Hats that have brims as a design feature will often call for a smaller needle for working the brim. This stiffens the fabric and helps make a sturdier brim, without having to reinforce the fabric.

Abbreviations

beg	beginning; begin; begins	**M1**	make one (increase)	**sl**	slip
bet	between	**M1R (L)**	make one right (left)	**sl st**	slip stitch (sl 1 st pwise unless otherwise indicated)
BO	bind off	**p**	purl		
CC	contrasting color	**p1f&b**	purl into front and back of same st	**ssk**	slip 1 kwise, slip 1 kwise, k2 sl sts tog tbl (decrease)
cm	centimeter(s)				
cn	cable needle	**p2tog**	purl two stitches together	**ssp**	slip 1 kwise, slip 1 kwise, p2 sl sts tog tbl (decrease)
CO	cast on	**patt(s)**	pattern(s)		
cont	continue(s); continuing	**pm**	place marker	**st(s)**	stitch(es)
dec(s)	decrease(s); decreasing	**psso**	pass slipped stitch over	**St st**	stockinette stitch
dpn	double-pointed needle(s)	**p2sso**	pass two slipped stitches over	**tbl**	through back loop
foll	following; follows			**tog**	together
g	gram(s)	**pwise**	purlwise	**WS**	wrong side
inc	increase(s); increasing	**RC**	right cross	**wyb**	with yarn in back
k	knit	**rem**	remain(s); remaining	**wyf**	with yarn in front
k1f&b	knit into front and back of same st	**rep**	repeat; repeating	**yo**	yarn over
		rev St st	reverse stockinette stitch	*****	repeat starting point (i.e., repeat from *)
k2tog	knit two stitches together	**rib**	ribbing		
kwise	knitwise	**rnd(s)**	round(s)	*** ***	repeat all instructions between asterisks
LC	left cross	**RS**	right side		
m(s)	marker(s)	**rev sc**	reverse single crochet	**( )**	alternate measurements and/or instructions
MC	main color	**sc**	single crochet		
mm	millimeter(s)	**sk**	skip	**[ ]**	instructions that are to be worked as a group a specified number of times

Glossary

Cast-Ons

Backward-Loop Cast-On

*Loop working yarn and place it on needle backward so that it doesn't unwind. Repeat from *.

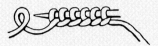

Cable Cast-On

If there are no stitches on the needles, make a slip-knot of working yarn and place it on the needle, then use the knitted method to cast on one more stitch—two stitches on needle. Hold needle with working yarn in your left hand. *Insert right needle between the first two stitches on left needle (**Figure 1**), wrap yarn around needle as if to knit, draw yarn through (**Figure 2**), and place new loop on left needle (**Figure 3**) to form a new stitch. Repeat from * for the desired number of stitches, always working between the first two stitches on the left needle.

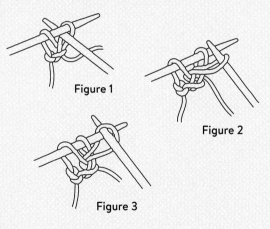

Figure 1

Figure 2

Figure 3

Emily Ocker Circular Beginning

This method for casting on for a circle in the round is invisible. Leaving a tail, make a large loop with the yarn. Hold the loop so that the crossing area of the loop is on the top and the tail is off to the left. With a double-pointed knitting needle, *reach inside the loop and pull the yarn coming from the ball through to make a stitch, then take the needle up over the top of the loop and yarn over; repeat from * until you have the desired number of stitches on the needle. Turn and knit one row. If you're casting on an even number of stitches, the sequence ends with a yarnover, and it will be difficult to keep from losing the last stitch. To solve this, pick up one extra stitch from the inside and then work these last two stitches together on the first row to get back to an even number of stitches. Divide the stitches evenly onto four double-pointed needles.

Knitted Cast-On

Place slipknot on left needle if there are no established stitches. *With right needle, knit into first stitch (or slipknot) on left needle (**Figure 1**) and place new stitch onto left needle (**Figure 2**). Repeat from *, always knitting into last stitch made.

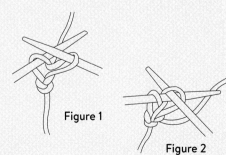

Figure 1

Figure 2

Provisional Cast-On

With waste yarn and crochet hook, make a loose crochet chain about four stitches more than you need to cast on. With knitting needle, working yarn, and beginning two stitches from end of chain, pick up and knit one stitch through the back loop of each crochet chain (**Figure 1**) for desired number of stitches. When you're ready to work in the opposite direction, pull out the crochet chain to expose live stitches (**Figure 2**).

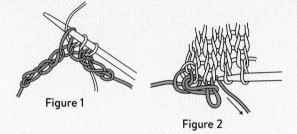

Figure 1

Figure 2

Long-Tail (Continental) Cast-On

Leaving a long tail (about ½" [1.3 cm] for each stitch to be cast on), make a slipknot and place on right needle. Place thumb and index finger of your left hand between the yarn ends so that working yarn is around your index finger and tail end is around your thumb and secure the yarn ends with your other fingers. Hold your palm upward, making a V of yarn (**Figure 1**). *Bring needle up through loop on thumb (**Figure 2**), catch first strand around index finger, and go back down through loop on thumb (**Figure 3**). Drop loop off thumb and, placing thumb back in V configuration, tighten resulting stitch on needle (**Figure 4**). Repeat from * for the desired number of stitches.

Figure 1

Figure 2

Figure 3

Figure 4

Turkish Cast-On

This method is worked by first wrapping the yarn around two parallel needles, then using a third needle to knit the loops on each of the two needles. The loops on one needle are the foundation for the instep, and the loops on the other needle are the foundation for the sole.

Hold two double-pointed needles parallel to each other. Leaving a 4" (10 cm) tail hanging to the front between the two needles, wrap the yarn around both needles from back to front half the number of times as desired stitches (four wraps shown here for eight stitches total), then bring the yarn forward between the needles (**Figure 1**).

Use a third needle to knit across the loops on the top needle, keeping the third needle on top of both the other needles when knitting the first stitch (**Figure 2**).

With the right side facing, rotate the two cast-on needles like the hands of a clock so that the bottom needle is on the top (**Figure 3**).

Knit across the loops on the new top needle (**Figure 4**).

Rotate the needles again and use a third needle to knit the first two stitches of the new top needle. There will now be two stitches each on two needles and four stitches on another needle (**Figure 5**).

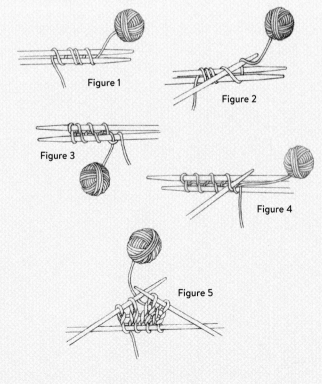

Figure 1

Figure 2

Figure 3

Figure 4

Figure 5

Bind-Offs

Decrease Bind-Off

VERSION A: Knitting through the back loops
This version gives a bind-off edge that looks just like a standard bind-off, but it is much stretchier.

STEP 1: Knit together the first two stitches on the left needle through the back loop (**Figure 1**).

STEP 2: Slip the new stitch on the right needle back to the left needle (**Figure 2**).

STEP 3: Repeat 1 and 2 until all stitches are bound off. Notice how the bind-off edge is nearly indistinguishable from your normal bind-off, but give it a tug and you'll see how much more flexible it is.

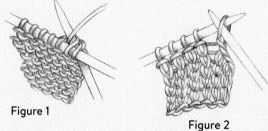

Figure 1

Figure 2

VERSION B: Knitting through the front loops

STEP 1: Knit together the first two stitches on the left needle (**Figure 3**).

STEP 2: Slip the new stitch on the right needle back to the left needle.

STEP 3: Repeat these two steps until all stitches are bound off.

In **Figure 4**, contrasting color yarn is used in the bind-off row so you can see the finished effect more clearly.

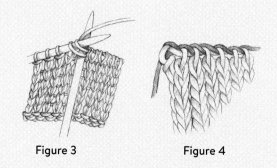

Figure 3

Figure 4

Sewn Bind-Off

This method, worked using a tapestry needle, forms an elastic edge that has a ropy appearance much like a purl row. It is ideal for finishing off garter stitch.

Cut the yarn, leaving a tail about three times the width of the knitting to be bound off, and thread the tail onto a tapestry needle.

Working from right to left, *insert the tapestry needle purlwise (from right to left) through the first two stitches on the left needle tip (**Figure 1**) and pull the yarn through. Bring tapestry needle through the first stitch again, but this time knitwise (from left to right; **Figure 2**), pull the yarn through, then slip this stitch off the knitting needle.

Repeat from * for the desired number of stitches.

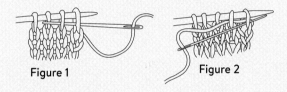

Figure 1

Figure 2

Three-Needle Bind-Off

Place the stitches to be joined onto two separate needles and hold the needles parallel so that the right sides of knitting face together. Insert a third needle into the first stitch on each of two needles (**Figure 1**) and knit them together as one stitch (**Figure 2**), *knit the next stitch on each needle the same way, then use the left needle tip to lift the first stitch over the second and off the needle (**Figure 3**). Repeat from * until no stitches remain on first two needles. Cut yarn and pull tail through last stitch to secure.

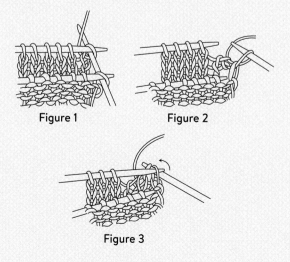

Figure 1

Figure 2

Figure 3

Increases

Bar Increase Knitwise (k1f&b)

Knit into a stitch but leave it on the left needle (**Figure 1**), then knit through the back loop of the same stitch (**Figure 2**) and slip the original stitch off the needle (**Figure 3**).

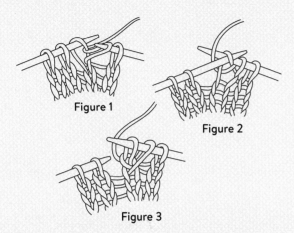

Figure 1

Figure 2

Figure 3

Raised (M1) Increases
Left Slant (M1L) and Standard M1

With left needle tip, lift strand between needles from front to back (**Figure 1**). Knit lifted loop through the back (**Figure 2**).

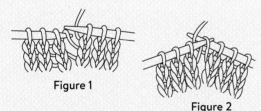

Figure 1

Figure 2

Right Slant (M1R)

With left needle tip, lift strand between needles from back to front (**Figure 1**). Knit lifted loop through the front (**Figure 2**).

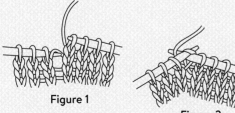

Figure 1

Figure 2

Purl (M1P)

For purl versions, work as above, purling lifted loop.

Yarnover Increase

This type of increase, formed by simply wrapping the yarn around the right needle tip, forms a decorative hole. The way that the yarn is wrapped depends upon whether it is preceded or followed by a knit or purl stitch.

BETWEEN TWO KNIT STITCHES: Wrap the yarn from front to back over the top of the right needle.

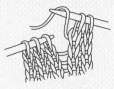

AFTER A KNIT STITCH AND BEFORE A PURL STITCH: Bring the yarn to the front under the right needle, around the top, then under the needle and to the front again.

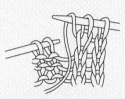

BETWEEN TWO PURL STITCHES: Bring the yarn from front to back over the top of the right needle, then around the bottom and to the front again.

AFTER A PURL STITCH AND BEFORE A KNIT STITCH: Bring the yarn from front to back over the top of the right needle.

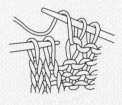

Decreases
Knit 2 Together (k2tog)

Knit two stitches together as if they were a single stitch.

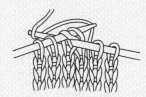

Knit 2 Together Through Back Loops (k2tog tbl)

Knit two stitches together through their back loops.

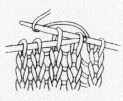

Knit 3 Together (k3tog)

Knit three stitches together as if they were a single stitch.

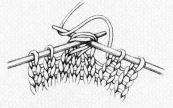

Purl 2 Together (p2tog)

Purl two stitches together as if they were a single stitch.

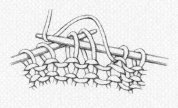

Slip, Slip, Knit (ssk)

Slip two stitches knitwise one at a time (**Figure 1**). Insert point of left needle into front of two slipped stitches and knit them together through back loops with right needle (**Figure 2**).

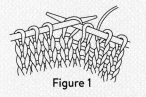

Figure 1

Figure 2

Slip, Slip, Purl (ssp)

Holding yarn in front, slip two stitches individually knitwise (**Figure 1**), then slip these two stitches back onto left needle (they will be twisted on the needle) and purl them together through their back loops (**Figure 2**).

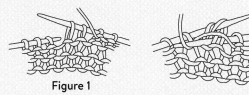

Figure 1

Figure 2

Short-Rows
Knit Side

Work to the turning point, slip next stitch purlwise to right needle. Bring yarn to front (**Figure 1**). Slip same stitch back to left needle (**Figure 2**). Turn work and bring yarn in position for next stitch, wrapping the slipped stitch as you do so.

note: *Hide wraps on a knit stitch when right side of piece is worked as a knit stitch. Leave wrap if the purl stitch shows on the right side.*

Hide wraps as follows: Knit stitch: On right side, work to just before wrapped stitch, insert right needle from front, under the wrap from bottom up, and then into wrapped stitch as usual. Knit them together, making sure the new stitch comes out under the wrap. Purl stitch: On wrong side, work to just before wrapped stitch. Insert right needle from back, under wrap from bottom up, and put on left needle. Purl lifted wrap and stitch together.

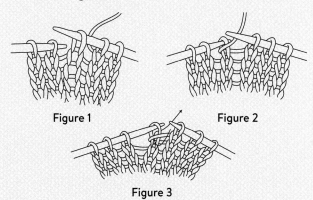
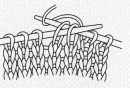

Figure 1

Figure 2

Figure 3

Purl Side

Work to the turning point, slip the next stitch purlwise to the right needle, bring the yarn to the back of the work (**Figure 1**), return the slipped stitch to the left needle, bring the yarn to the front between the needles (**Figure 2**), and turn the work so that the knit side is facing—one stitch has been wrapped and the yarn is correctly positioned to knit the next stitch. To hide the wrap on a subsequent purl row, work to the wrapped stitch, use the tip of the right needle to pick up the wrap from the back, place it on the left needle (**Figure 3**), then purl it together with the wrapped stitch.

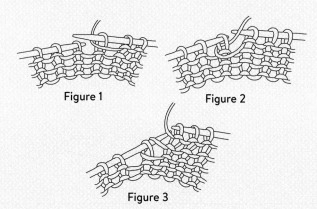

Figure 1　　　　Figure 2

Figure 3

Wrap & Turn (w&t)

Work to the turning point, slip next stitch purlwise to rightneedle (**Figure 1**). Bring yarn to front (**Figure 2**). Slip same stitch back to left needle (**Figure 3**). Turn work and bring yarn in position for next stitch, wrapping the stitch as you do so.

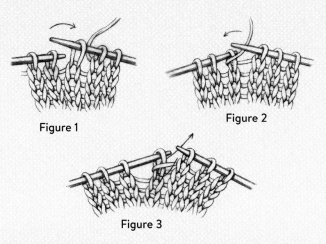

Figure 1　　　　Figure 2

Figure 3

note: *Hide wraps in a knit stitch when right side of piece is worked in a knit stitch. Leave wrap if the purl stitch shows on right side.*

Hide wraps as follows:

KNIT STITCH: On right side, work to just before wrapped stitch. Insert right needle from front, under the wrap from bottom up, and then into wrapped stitch as usual. Knit them together, making sure new stitch comes out under wrap.

PURL STITCH: On wrong side, work to just before wrapped stitch. Insert right needle from back, under wrap from bottom up, and put on left needle. Purl them together.

Grafting
Kitchener Stitch (St st Grafting)

STEP 1: Bring threaded needle through front stitch as if to purl and leave stitch on needle (**Figure 1**).

STEP 2: Bring threaded needle through back stitch as if to knit and leave stitch on needle (**Figure 2**).

STEP 3: Bring threaded needle through first front stitch as if to knit and slip this stitch off needle. Bring threaded needle through next front stitch as if to purl and leave stitch on needle (**Figure 3**).

STEP 4: Bring threaded needle through first back stitch as if to purl (as illustrated), slip this stitch off, bring needle through next back stitch as if to knit, leave this stitch on needle (**Figure 4**).

Repeat Steps 3 and 4 until no stitches remain on needles.

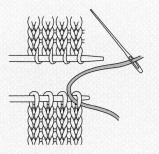

Figure 1

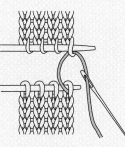

Figure 2

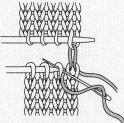

Figure 3

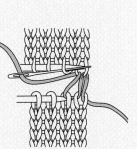

Figure 4

Seams
Mattress Stitch Seam

With RS of knitting facing, use threaded needle to pick up one bar between first two stitches on one piece (**Figure 1**), then corresponding bar plus the bar above it on other piece (**Figure 2**). *Pick up next two bars on first piece, then next two bars on other (**Figure 3**). Repeat from * to end of seam, finishing by picking up last bar (or pair of bars) at the top of first piece.

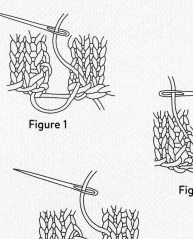

Figure 1

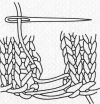

Figure 2

Figure 3

Crochet
Crochet Chain (ch)

Make a slipknot and place it on crochet hook if there isn't a loop already on the hook. *Yarn over hook and draw through loop on hook. Repeat from * for the desired number of stitches. To fasten off, cut yarn and draw end through last loop formed.

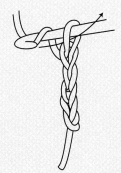

Pick Up and Knit

Pick Up and Knit along CO or BO Edge

With right side facing and working from right to left, insert the tip of the needle into the center of the stitch below the bind-off or cast-on edge (**Figure 1**), wrap yarn around needle, and pull through a loop (**Figure 2**). Pick up one stitch for every existing stitch.

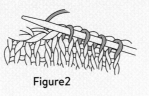

Figure 1   Figure2

Whipstitch

With right side of work facing and working one stitch in from the edge, bring threaded needle out from back to front along edge of knitted piece.

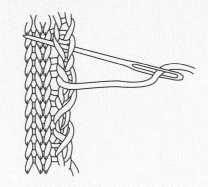

Buttonholes

Three-Stitch One-Row Buttonhole

Bring the yarn to the front of the work, slip the next stitch purlwise, then return the yarn to the back. *Slip the next stitch, pass the second stitch over the slipped stitch and drop it off the needle. Repeat from * once more (**Figure 1**). Slip the last stitch on the right needle to the left needle and turn the work around. Bring the working yarn to the back, [insert the right needle between the first and second stitches on the left needle; **Figure 2**), draw up a loop and place it on the left needle] 3 times. Turn the work around. With the yarn in back, slip the first stitch and pass the extra cast-on stitch over it (**Figure 3**) and off the needle to complete the buttonhole.

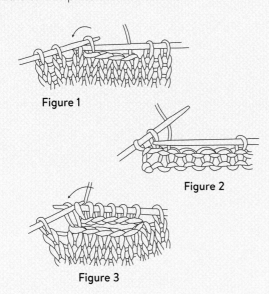

Figure 1

Figure 2

Figure 3

Index

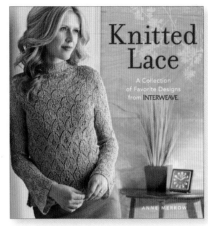
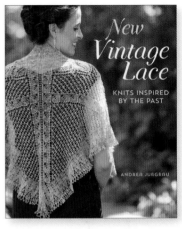